TABLE OF CONTENTS

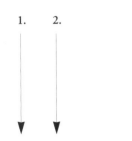
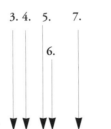

1450   1585

TABLE OF CONTENTS

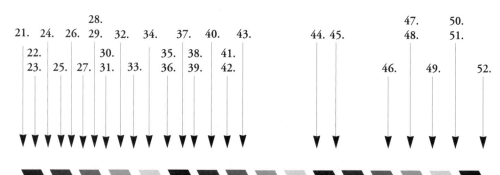

1586   **1640**

TABLE OF CONTENTS

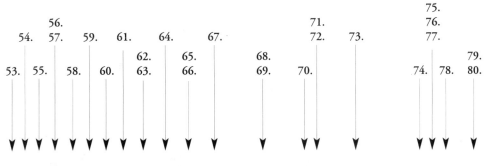

1641

1700

TABLE OF CONTENTS

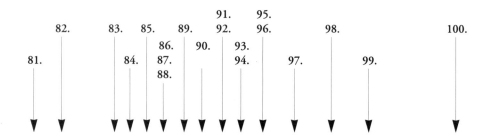

1701

1750

INTRODUCTION

First there was the land: enormous forests, long river valleys, tremendous mountains and prairies. North America teamed with wildlife. It was a paradise.

Next came the immigrants from Asia. Known today as Native Americans, they crossed the land bridge from Russia to Alaska to reach North America thousands of years ago. They traveled to the south and east, and over the centuries gave rise to spectacularly different cultures, from the southwest Pueblo Indians to the northeast Iroquois.

During the thousands of years that passed, the continent remained largely unchanged. Then the immigrants from Europe arrived. They were Spanish, French, Dutch, English, and Swedish, explorers and navigators, seekers of religious freedom, fortune hunters, and merchants. Leaders such as Jacques Cartier, Juan de Onate, and William Bradford led the way and created settlements that became Nouvelle France, Neuvo Mexico, and New England. Later, Nieuw Nederlansch (New Netherland) and Nova Swerige (New Sweden) were established by people such as Peter Stuyvesant and Peter Minuit.

The second and third generations of European colonists fought long and bloody wars against the Native Americans. The Pequot War, King Philip's War, and Pope's Rebellion are testimony to the violence that followed the European occupation of the eastern fringes of North America.

The colonists also fought each other. New Sweden was swallowed up by New Netherland, which was in turn devoured by English soldiers serving the Duke of York, and so became New York. By 1690, there were only three groups of Europeans left: the French in Canada and Acadia, the English from Maine to Carolina, and the Spanish in Florida and New Mexico.

The fourth and fifth generation colonial Americans intensified trade. Tobacco in Virginia, rice and cotton in Carolina, molasses in New England, cod in Acadia, and beaver skins in Canada all became prized possessions that brought wealth to the colonists. The desire to produce more cotton, tobacco, and sugar resulted in the need for unpaid labor, and so, unwilling immigrants to North America—black Africans—were forced to toil as slaves.

At the same time, the European Enlightenment found its way to North America. James Logan and Benjamin Franklin put Philadelphia on the intellectual map, and colonial Virginians began to educate their sons at home with private tutors.

In the mid-18th century, France and Great Britain went to war to determine which nation would dominate North America. In 1759, Britain and its colonists defeated the French and captured Canada. Spain entered the war on behalf of the French, and quickly lost Florida to the British.

When the dust settled in 1763, Great Britain appeared to have triumphed everywhere. Only the Native Americans beyond the Appalachian Mountains posed any threat to British control. For all that, the land remained much the same as it always had. Ninety percent of the continent was inhabited only by native tribes, and no European had traveled all the way across North America north of Mexico. However, change was on the way. The American Revolution would remove the British and create a new sovereign power, the United States of America. During the next century, westward expansion and the Industrial Revolution would harness the power of America's rivers, create cities—and forever change the landscape that had once been an Eden.

1. John Cabot
(c. 1450–1498)

If any single European can be credited with opening the door to Canada, it was **John Cabot**. While there is almost no historical documentation about Cabot—no signature, description, or portrait—it is known that his real name was Giovanni Caboto, and he was born in the mid-15th century in Genoa, Italy.

The first documented reference to Cabot dates from when he became a Venetian citizen in 1475. He was a successful mariner-merchant, married an Italian woman, and by 1484 he was buying and selling real estate in Venice. It is known that he appeared in England no later than 1495. On March 4, 1496, King **Henry VII** granted permission to Cabot and his three sons — Lewis, Sebastian and Santius — to lead an expedition to the **New World**.

Cabot at Newfoundland

Cabot had settled in **Bristol**, one of the major ports of England and home to some of the most adventurous mariners of that time. Here he acquired some financial backers and a small ship, the Matthew. Cabot sailed, in May 1497 with a mainly British crew. Although he had little more than a compass and a quadrant for navigation, he was an experienced sailor and made good time crossing the Atlantic Ocean.

On June 24, the Matthew made landfall someplace along the northeastern coast of **Canada**, most likely in **Newfoundland**. Cabot went ashore briefly, then sailed down the coast and back. He made a remarkably fast return voyage to England, leaving Newfoundland on July 20 and arriving safely back at Bristol on August 6.

Cabot brought back reports of the New World and its resources such as codfish and tall trees that could be used for ship masts. He was immediately rewarded by the King of England and given a new royal grant. This time he was authorized to lead a fleet of well-provisioned ships to this new land to found a colony. Cabot's five ships set off from Bristol in May 1498. One, damaged by a storm, returned to Ireland shortly thereafter. The other four ships disappeared. Whether they went down at sea or arrived in North America and then met difficulties is not known, but Cabot was never heard of again.

Cabot, like Columbus, mistakenly thought he had found some new route to China and the East Indies. Although Cabot's voyage did not lead to any immediate gain, the success of his first trip served as a major inspiration for the colonization of North America that soon followed. In 1997, the Canadian maritime provinces celebrated the 500th anniversary of Cabot's arrival in the New World.

2. Ponce de Leon
(c. 1460–1521)

Juan Ponce de Leon was born into a distinguished noble family in Santervas, Spain. He joined the army and fought to drive the Moors out of Granada, their last outpost in Spain in 1492. He probably sailed on Columbus's second voyage in 1493 and stayed briefly at the Spanish settlement on **Hispaniola**. In 1502, de Leon was called back to Hispaniola to help put down a rebellion by the native inhabitants in Haiti, where he remained and became the deputy governor in 1504.

De Leon first explored **Puerto Rico** in 1508, and returned to Hispaniola with some gold given him by a native chief. In 1509, he became governor of Spain's colony in Puerto Rico. He secured Spain's military dominance there and soon became one of the richest and most powerful Spaniards in the New World. When political rivals managed to have him removed from office in 1512, he decided to seek new adventures.

De Leon persuaded King **Ferdinand** to give him permission to find and colonize an island near Puerto Rico that the Indians called **Bimini**. De Leon was influenced by legends that there was a magical spring, whose waters restored one's youth. He set off in 1513 and explored what became the **Bahamas**. In April of that year, he landed on what he believed was another island, naming it "**Florida**," Spanish for "full of flowers."

De Leon had probably landed near the site of modern-day **St. Augustine**. He explored the coast all the way south, around the tip, and part way up the western coast. He engaged in skirmishes with native fighters, and after a major engagement that June, he sailed away from Florida. After cruising in the Caribbean, he returned to Puerto Rico. Proud

Ponce de Leon

of his discoveries, he sailed to Spain in 1514. King Ferdinand commissioned de Leon to colonize Florida and Bimini; he was also ordered to get rid of the Carib Indians who inhabited the **West Indies**.

De Leon returned to the West Indies and proceeded to kill many natives. Finally, in February, 1521, he sailed from Puerto Rico with 200 men and supplies to colonize Florida. The party landed on Florida's west coast, probably near modern-day Charlotte Harbor. Native forces immediately attacked them. De Leon was wounded by an arrow, and he and his men fled to Cuba, where de Leon died of his wound.

Alvar Nuñez Cabeza de Vaca

If ever there was a conquistador who deserves to be known as a survivor, it is **Alvar Nuñez Cabeza de Vaca**. Born in the region of Spain near Portugal, de Vaca was named treasurer of a 600-man expedition which sailed from Cuba to explore Florida in 1528.

The Spaniards landed near **Tampa Bay** in April, 1528 and, lured by the Indians' tales of riches, made their way north to the country of the **Apalachee Indians**. Under constant attack, the Spaniards made their way down to the Gulf of Mexico near modern-day Apalachicola, Florida. Here they built five barges, and in September, the 242 survivors—including de Vaca—set sail.

As the expedition traveled along the north coast of the gulf, one of the barges became separated. The other four barges sailed on until they were struck by a hurricane off the northeastern coast of Texas. Eighty survivors made their way ashore to what became **Galveston**, Texas. De Vaca—half drowned

and naked—found himself on a small island just south, where he was soon joined by two other Spaniards and a slave, whose barge had also capsized.

Cahoques Indians immediately imprisoned the men, and for the next eight years de Vaca and the others remained among various Indian tribes. Cabeza de Vaca was given many tasks to perform for the Indians. He served as a medicine man, although his medical "treatment" consisted mainly of blessing, breathing on, and praying for the sick. He was also forced to perform menial jobs, such as bringing water and wood, dragging canoes, and helping set up houses when the Indians moved to a new place.

In 1532, de Vaca and the three other captives were taken off the island and moved about 100 miles down the coast to the Matagorda Peninsula. They were then turned over as slaves to a tribal chief. The four men remained there until 1534 when they were finally able to escape into the Texas wilderness

Making their way across hundreds of miles of what would become Texas, **New Mexico** and **Arizona**, they began an incredible 17-month journey. With no supplies, they went barefoot and virtually naked much of the way.

In February 1536, they made their way down into northern Mexico where they came across a small company of Spanish soldiers. After recovering their strength, they went on to Mexico City, arriving that June. They were received with both astonishment and admiration, and tales of their adventures soon spread.

De Vaca returned to Spain in 1537 where he wrote an account of his experiences. The book, published in 1542, proved to the Spanish that there existed a land mass north of New Spain (Mexico) much greater than they had believed.

4. Jacques Cartier
(1491–1557)

Jacques **Cartier** was born in 1491 at St. Malo, a French port along the coast of Britanny. Little is known of Cartier's early years but he seems to have become prosperous through his skill as a master navigator. What is known for certain is that in 1534, Cartier was commissioned by King **Francis I** of France to sail to North America. His mission was not only to find gold and other precious metals but to find the fabled "**Northwest Passage**" from the Atlantic Ocean to Asia and the East Indies.

In April 1534, Cartier sailed from St. Malo with two ships. They arrived in the **Gulf of St. Lawrence**, and for the next 12 weeks they explored the gulf and its various islands. They went ashore frequently and hunted birds and mammals. They also met some Native Americans with whom they exchanged goods and gifts. Since Cartier had found neither gold nor a passage way to China, he needed some proof of his visit to show his king on his return to France. Cartier convinced one chieftain, **Donnaconna**, to let him take his two teenage sons to France, on condition that they would be safely returned. Early in August, Cartier and his men returned to St. Malo, where their tales of plentiful food and gentle natives encouraged many to want to settle this new world.

In May 1535, Cartier set sail with three ships. With Donnaconna's sons as guides, he sailed up the St. Lawrence River and visited the Indian village of Stadacona at the site of what would later become **Quebec City**. Here the two Indian boys were reunited with their father. Cartier then sailed on to visit the large village named Hochelaga at the site of what would become **Montreal**. With winter closing in, the French chose to stay near Stadacona. During the miserable winter, 25 of the 110 in their party died from scurvy and other ailments. The others survived only because the Indians showed them how to brew tea from tree bark.

Returning to France in 1536, Cartier was commissioned for a third time by King Francis I. In May 1541, Cartier sailed with five ships and at least 200 people, including 50 convicts who were forced to emigrate. Cartier's expedition easily made it to the St. Lawrence and to Stadacona, but relations with the natives quickly deteriorated. Over the winter of 1541–1542, many of the French were either killed or died from scurvy. In June 1542, Cartier abandoned his attempt at establishing a colony near Quebec and returned to France. He lived out his final years as a respected mariner and explorer of Canada.

Jacques Cartier

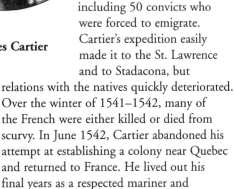

5. Hernando de Soto
(c. 1498–1542)

Hernando de Soto

Hernando de Soto participated in Spanish campaigns in the West Indies, Panama and Nicaragua from 1514 to 1530. He joined **Francisco Pizarro** in the conquest of Peru in 1532, and remained there until 1536, returning to Spain as a wealthy man.

In 1537, de Soto was named governor of the Spanish colony in **Cuba** and captain-general of **Florida**. He went to Cuba in 1538 and a year later set off to explore Florida and its unknown borderlands. Like many of the conquistadors, de Soto was inspired by a love of adventure, as well as a desire to become rich.

De Soto organized the expedition with some 600 men, and in May 1539, he landed on the coast of Florida near modern-day Tampa Bay. For the next three years, de Soto would lead his men on one of the greatest odysseys of North American history.

De Soto moved quickly up the Florida coast into north-central Florida, where his mistreatment of the **Apalachee Indians** led them to harass his men during the winter there. In March, 1540, the Spaniards moved north into Georgia and across the Savannah River into South Carolina. They then marched into the Blue Ridge Mountains and the southwestern corner of North Carolina and the southeastern corner of Tennessee. Throughout this time, de Soto and his men constantly stole food and other supplies from the local tribes, brutalized the men and women, and generally convinced the Native Americans that the Europeans brought only trouble.

The Spanish then turned south and came down into Alabama, following the Alabama River to a place known as **Mabila**, near modern-day Mobile. There they fought a major battle with hostile Indians, in which the Spaniards killed more than 2,000 men. De Soto was wounded and 18 of his companions were killed.

On May 9, 1541, de Soto and his party became the first Europeans to see the **Mississippi River**. They constructed barges and went north into Arkansas where they spent the winter of 1541–1542. In March 1542, they set off eastward to make their way back to the Mississippi River. By this time, de Soto had contracted a fever and died on May 21.

De Soto's men buried his body in the Mississippi so that the Native Americans would not discover that the Spanish leader was dead. The surviving Spaniards built boats in which they floated down the Mississippi River and eventually arrived in **Mexico** in September, 1543.

While De Soto's expedition failed to achieve its original goals, his journey indicated to other explorers that North America was there for exploration and perhaps colonization.

6. Estevanico
(c. 1500-1539)

Estevan, or **Estevanico**, Spanish for "Little Steven" was apparently from Morocco, which means he may have been of mixed African and Arabic descent. He is often referred to as a slave, but this term can be misleading. He may well have been captured by the Spanish in some battle and then enslaved, but like many such captives, he probably became a trusted free servant.

Estevanico was attached to an expedition that sailed from Spain in 1527, the same one that included **Alvar Nuñez Cabeza de Vaca** (see no. 3). Like de Vaca, he was among the 80 survivors of the storm that blew them onto the future site of **Galveston**, Texas. Eventually, Estevanico, de Vaca, and two other Spaniards found themselves being held captive by a tribe of **Cahoques Indians**. For the next several years, the four remained among various Indian tribes on an island south of the Galveston site.

Finally, in September 1534, Estevanico, de Vaca, and the two Spaniards made their escape. For 17 months, they walked across what would become Texas, New Mexico and Arizona in one of the most harrowing journeys ever made. By the time the four men arrived in Mexico City in June 1536, Estevanico had long since ceased to be regarded as an inferior slave.

Indeed, Viceroy **Mendoza** assigned Estevanico to guide the expedition led by an experienced Franciscan priest-explorer, **Fray Marcos de Niza**. The goal was to seek out the fabled seven **Cities of Cibola**. Some Europeans claimed that hundreds of years earlier the Portuguese had gone to the New World and established these cities that were supposedly full of gold. The de Niza expedition set out in March 1539. They went into New Mexico and Fray Marcos sent Estevanico ahead with some Indian guides. He was instructed to mark his trail with crosses; the larger the size of the "city" he passed through, the larger the cross.

Fray Marcos followed this trail for two months. The large crosses he found suggested Estevanico must have found great cities. Messengers returning from Estevanico confirmed this. That May, Fray Marcos received word that Estevanico was killed by Indians at the **Zuni Hawikuh** pueblo near modern-day Gallup, **New Mexico**. He was probably killed by the Indians to prevent him from leading more Europeans—who were going to bring trouble—into the area. In any case, Fray Marcos did not try to enter Hawikuh and returned to Mexico City. Like so many of the early explorers to enter North America, Estevanico had failed in his original goals, but he helped pave the way for future expeditions.

Spaniards invading Indian village

Francisco Vásquez de Coronado
(1510–1554)

Coronado and his conquistidors

Perhaps the man who most embodies the best and the worst qualities of the conquistadors is **Francisco Vásquez de Coronado** from Salamanca, Spain. Coronado went to Mexico in 1535 and became governor of the northern Mexican province of **Neuva Galicia** in 1538.

Early Spanish conquistadoes had heard from Indians rumors of fabulous cities and riches to the north. There was one particularly intriguing story about the Seven Golden Cities of Cibola. These rumors increased after **Alvar Nuñez Cabeza de Vaca** (see no. 3) returned to Mexico in 1536 from his incredible adventures. **Fray Marcos de Niza** aroused further interest when he returned from his expedition of 1538-1539, reporting great wealth to be found to the north. The Spanish leaders in **Mexico City** were eager to learn more, and it fell to Coronado to head a new and more ambitious expedition. Coronado organized a group of 400 European men, women and children, 1,300 Indians, and many cattle, sheep, and pigs. The expedition set off in February 1540.

Coronado and his men proceeded into southwestern Arizona. They arrived at the great **Zuni Indian** pueblo, a communal village, in Hawikuh in New Mexico. There was no gold here, however, only hostile natives. The Zuni revolted when Coronado tried to impose Spanish rule over the pueblo, but the Spanish soon triumphed. Meanwhile, Coronado dispatched small scouting parties into other regions. Some went to the pueblos of New Mexico and Arizona. Another party, led by Captain **Lopez de Cardenas**, proceeded west and became the first Europeans to see the **Grand Canyon**. A third group explored the region around Albuquerque and marched through the upper **Rio Grande** and eastward along the Pecos River. The expeditions returned to the pueblos near Santa Fe, where Coronado gathered all his men to spend the winter of 1540–1541.

Coronado's men treated the inhabitants of the pueblos terribly, stealing their food and possessions. This led to fights throughout the winter. At one point, Coronado ordered 200 Indians burned at the stake. Then in April 1541, he set off with part of his group to find the city of Quivira, the fabled city of riches. Proceeding with only 30 men, Coronado reached Quivira, most likely modern-day Wichita, **Kansas**. It was little more than a village. Coronado left the region in August, 1541 and spent the winter near Albuquerque.

Along the way, Coronado had been injured in a horse accident. Ailing and disillusioned, he led his expedition back to Mexico City, arriving there in July 1542. The Spanish authorities charged Coronado with mistreatment of the Native Americans and the general failures of his expedition, but he was found innocent. Coronado died in Mexico City in 1554.

8. Pedro Menéndez de Avilés
(1519–1574)

Pedro Menéndez de Avilés was born in Aviles, Spain. At age 14, he ran away to become a sailor. By his early 20s, he owned his own ship. For the next 20 years he gained both a reputation and fortune by attacking pirates off the coast of Spain and making trade voyages to the West Indies. He played a major role in establishing the route and schedule under which Spain sent fleets of ships to and from the New World.

By 1565, Catholic Spain was becoming greatly concerned about reports of the French presence on the southeastern coast of North America. In particular, the Spanish did not like the idea of Protestants anywhere near what they regarded as their territory. King **Philip II** of Spain gave Menéndez a contract to serve as captain-general of **Florida**. The mission was clear: Menéndez was not only to establish Spanish settlements, he was to expel all other Europeans from the region, in particular the French. He was also to establish forts that would protect the sea route for the treasure-laden Spanish ships making their way back to Spain.

Menéndez and his fleet set sail in June 1565. That September, they encountered the French ships of **Jean Ribaut** (see no. 9) off the coast of Florida. The French fled to the safety of **Fort Caroline**, so Menéndez landed about 40 miles south. On September 20, after he discovered that the French had split their forces, Menéndez approached Fort Caroline from the rear. During the brutal attack that ensued, the Spanish killed or executed some 132 Frenchmen. Forty-five Frenchmen escaped; women and children were captured and returned to France.

Menéndez took over the fort and renamed it **San Mateo**. In the following weeks, he and his men killed most of the French who had been away from the fort and later returned, although he spared the few who could prove

they were Roman Catholics. Menéndez's actions effectively ended French attempts to settle in that part of North America.

Menéndez was a man of incredible energy. He immediately set about to secure Spain's presence in the southeast. In 1565, at the spot where he had originally landed, Menéndez established a fort he named **San Augustin**, at the site of modern-day St. Augustine. This became the core of the first European city established in North America. He established another major fort at **St. Elena** in modern-day **South Carolina**, and on the west coast of Florida he established a military-mission post, **San Antonio de Carlos**. Jesuit missionaries arrived in Florida in 1567 to convert the native inhabitants.

Menéndez returned to Spain in 1567 where he was granted many honors for establishing the Spanish presence in the New World.

Pedro Menéndez de Avilés

9. Jean Ribaut
(1520–1565)

Jean Ribaut was born in Dieppe, France, and rose to become a prominent officer in the French navy. Ribaut was also a devout Protestant at a time when there was increasing friction between France's Roman Catholic majority and the Protestant minority, known as **Huguenots**.

The Huguenots developed a colonizing expedition that Ribaut was chosen to lead. Ribaut chose as his second in command another Protestant, **Rene Goulaine de Laudonniere**. The expedition sailed from France in 1562. They landed at the mouth of the St. Johns River in northern **Florida** where they erected a stone column to commemorate their visit. They then sailed north to a place they named **Port Royal Sound**, in modern-day **South Carolina**. There, on what became known as Parris Island, they built a small fort, named it **Charlesfort**, and planned their settlement.

Leaving settlers behind, Ribaut and Laudonniere returned to France for supplies, but were delayed in returning to Charlesfort. Seeking refuge from the religious wars then raging in France, Ribaut fled to England, where he published an English translation of his report about the colony. Meanwhile, the French colonists at Charlesfort were so desperate for food that they abandoned the settlement in 1563. They constructed a crude boat and set sail for France; after several weeks of drifting in the Atlantic, they were picked up by an English ship and eventually returned to France.

Ribaut and Laudonniere organized another expedition. Laudonniere went out with the colonists in 1564 and built **Fort Caroline** near the mouth of the St. Johns River. Ribaut arrived in August 1565 with more supplies and reinforcements.

Unfortunately, the Spanish under **Pedro Menéndez de Aviles** (see no. 8) arrived at the same time and attacked the fort. The French had foolishly divided their forces and those in the fort had no chance against the Spanish. Nearly 132 Frenchmen were killed by the Spanish; another 45 escaped, among them Laudonniere. He got to a French ship offshore and eventually made his way back to France.

Ribaut was not so lucky. He had not been at Fort Caroline when it was taken by the Spanish. However, he and his force of about 350 men were discovered by Spanish troops on a beach near **St. Augustin**. While the French were negotiating their surrender, some 200 of them fled into the wilderness. Ribaut led the remaining 150 to surrender, believing they would be shown mercy. Instead, the Spanish executed all but 15 who were able to establish that they were Roman Catholics. Ribaut was brutally murdered.

Although Ribaut had failed, his vision of a haven for religious dissenters would be followed by others, including the **Pilgrims**.

Jean Ribaut

16

Juan de Oñate was the son of a wealthy and prominent Spanish Basque family in the colony of **Nueva España** (New Spain), or Mexico. Onate added to his status by marrying Dona Isabel de Tolosa, the granddaughter of **Cortes** and his Indian princess, and the great-granddaughter of **Montezuma**, the Aztec ruler.

Oñate served as a soldier on the northern frontier of New Spain for 20 years. The Spanish were interested in further exploring and exploiting this territory north of Mexico, and Oñate made a contract with the viceroy of Mexico in 1595. At his own expense, Oñate organized a party of 500 Spanish-Mexicans—supplied with 80 wagons loaded with provisions and 7,000 head of livestock—to search for the rich mines rumored to exist in the region and to settle there.

This great expedition set out from Mexico in February 1598, and by May, it crossed the Rio Grande River at modern-day El Paso, Texas. The group moved slowly up the river valley and into the territory of the **Pueblo Indians**. In July, the settlers arrived at their first major pueblo, the **Okhe Pueblo** in the Esanola Valley. Oñate decided to call this place **San Juan de los Caballeros**, and designated it as the capital of the Spanish colony.

Oñate tried to conquer as many neighboring Indian pueblos as possible, and he showed almost no compassion or tolerance for the Native Americans. He raided the pueblos, robbed the men, and raped their women.

The worst example of Oñate's cruelty occurred at the **Acoma Pueblo**. His party so abused the inhabitants that some of them rose up and killed 13 of the Spaniards. Oñate

Pueblo in New Mexico

decided to punish the Indians, so he used his cannon to demolish the pueblo. Many Native Americans were killed; more than 500 men, women, and children were placed in captivity.

Oñate had been sending back glowing reports about life in the new colony—**New Mexico**—and that attracted many new settlers from Mexico. However, in fact, life in the colony was difficult. Oñate was coming under increasing criticism for his mismanagement of the colony, while he complained that he was spending too much of his personal fortune. Finally, in August, 1608, Oñate renounced his official positions.

Back in Mexico City, Oñate was formally accused of mismanagement, cruelty to the Indians and his fellow colonists, and of making false reports. His punishment included fines, the loss of his titles, and permanent banishment from New Mexico. In the years that followed, Oñate worked to clear his name and had some success before he died. However, history still remembers him as a terrible Spanish colonial leader in the New World.

11. Powhatan
(c. 1550–1618)

Wahunsonacock, whom the English called **Powhatan** for his birthplace, was a member of the **Renape** tribe of **Algonquin Indians**. Powhatan evidently inherited his chief's status in the Renape fashion, through his mother. He attained his full power as a chieftain and priest by the force of his personality, his energy, and ultimately, his willingness to employ force. In the several decades before the English arrived to colonize his territory, Powhatan imposed his power over 28 loosely related tribes living in 200 villages around **Chesapeake Bay**.

Powhatan would be described by Captain **John Smith** as a "tall, well-proportioned man… His age is near 60, of a very able and hardy body to endure any labour." Another English colonist wrote that Powhatan "hath been a strong and able savage, sinewy, active and of a daring spirit, vigilant, ambitious." He surrounded himself with 40 or 50 bodyguards and never slept without 4 men guarding his house. He also maintained a large family; he was said to have had at least 12 wives, and he fathered at least 20 sons and 10 daughters.

When English colonists first arrived in May, 1607, Powhatan was wary because English sea captains had already been seizing Indians as slaves. However, he chose to let the English begin their settlement at **Jamestown**. The settlers' first months were disastrous due to the climate and the lack of proper water and food. In the summer of 1608, Smith took charge and organized the colonists more efficiently. Smith suffered a wound, however, and had to return to England in 1609.

Powhatan allowed the English to settle in, but he remained on his guard. Smith later claimed that Powhatan told him that he had at first assumed that the English had come merely to trade, but he now realized they intended to settle permanently. Although Powhatan did not wage an all-out war against the English, he did not stop members of his tribes from frequently attacking them. Between 1610 and 1613 he carried out a series of attacks against the English and seized some of them as prisoners. He refused to release them when the English took his daughter **Pocahontas** as a hostage in 1613 (see no. 30).

Powhatan maintained an uneasy relationship with the English settlers until his death. Leadership of the tribes then passed to his half-brother **Opechancanough**.

Powhatan

18

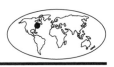

12. Opechancanough
(c. 1556–1646)

C.Smith taketh the King of Pamavnkee prisoner 1608

Opechancanough and John Smith

While Chief **Powhatan** (see no. 11) had a mixed relationship with the English settlers at Jamestown, his half-brother **Opechancanough** (o-pech-en-ka-no) left no uncertainty about his attitude toward the colonists.

Little is known about Opechancanough's early years, but some evidence suggests that his father was a Mexican Indian, possibly a survivor of the Indians brought into North America by **Hernando de Soto** (see no. 5). Others believe that Opechancanough himself may have been taken to Florida and even Spain at one point. In any case, he became the chief of the **Pamunkey** branch of the **Renape Indians**. The Pamunkey were subject to Powhatan and his confederacy, but Opechancanough evidently enjoyed some special powers because of his close relationship with Powhatan.

When the English arrived at **Jamestown** in 1607, Opechancaough and his fellow Native Americans were already aware of the threats posed by the Europeans who had been exploring North America for a century. In December 1607, Opechancanough captured Captain **John Smith** for entering his territory (see no. 16). However, the two men reach an uneasy truce, and during the next decades, Opechancanough apparently helped the English against rival tribes. Still, he never really accepted the ever-expanding European presence in his land.

After the death of Powhatan in 1618, Opechancanough became the main chief of his brother's confederacy. Before long, his attitude toward the settlers became very hostile. When the English killed a warrior and prophet named **Nemattanow** in 1622, Opechancanough called for a surprise attack on the colonists in **Virginia**. The organized Indian attacks on the settlements along the James River killed 347 English people—nearly one-third of the colony. This led to all-out war, but by the following year, the English had received reinforcements, and they forced Opechancanough to settle for a truce.

For the next 20 years, various incidents and skirmishes arose between the Native Americans and the English in Virginia. However, even though there was no major conflict, the Indians could see that the English were rapidly expanding their settlements. In 1644, the now aged and nearly blind Opechancanough called for another surprise attack on the English. The Indians rose up in March and killed 500 colonists, but this time Opechancanough was captured and brought to Jamestown. The aged Indian chieftain was then killed by angry guards while being held in a jail. His death ended the Powhatan confederacy's war against the English, and the settlers proceeded to expand their colony.

13. John White
(c. 1557–c.1593)

John White is one of the great "mystery men" of the early colonial period. Little is known or agreed upon about White's life, but he left some of the most vivid images of the earliest colonial period in North America.

White first surfaces in English history around 1575, when he was accepted as a member of the Painter-Stainers' Company of London, something similar to a union of professional painters. In 1577 he joined an expedition organized by Martin Frobisher for Frobisher's second voyage to the New World. The expedition spent that summer cruising around what is now known as Frobisher Bay, just to the north of the Hudson Strait. During those weeks, White made drawings and paintings of the Eskimos, the earliest known pictures of those people.

In 1585, White joined an expedition organized by Sir Walter Raleigh. The goal was to establish on the North American coast an English colony to be named "Virginia" for Queen Elizabeth I, the "Virgin Queen." Some 108 English settlers landed at Roanoke Island, along the coast of modern-day Virginia. White made some remarkable drawings of the natives and their settlements, then returned to England when the colonization ended because of conflict between the settlers and the natives.

In 1587, a new expedition with 117 people sailed to North America to establish a new colony, and this time John White went along as its governor. The group arrived at Roanoke in July, and in August, White's daughter Eleanor Dare, gave birth to the first child born to the English in North America; the baby was christened Virginia Dare. The following year, the colonists persuaded White that he should return to England to gain more supplies for their struggling colony. Again, White took back to Europe valuable drawings and maps of the New World.

White occupied himself in London, trying to organize a relief expedition; however, his return was delayed by England's war against the Spanish Armada in 1588. White finally set sail in March, 1590. When his group arrived at Roanoke Island several months later, they found no one. Instead, in the ruins of the settlement, they found the word "CROATOAN" carved onto a tree. This referred to a nearby island, but before White's group could visit there, a storm drove them out to sea.

The fate of "the lost colony" remains unknown. Some people believe the colonists were wiped out by the natives or by the Spanish, but others believe that they gradually joined with some friendly tribes and were simply absorbed by them. While nothing is known of John White's later years, his drawings and paintings remain as unique evidence of the earliest phase of North American colonization.

White finds " Croatoan" carved onto a tree

14. Samuel de Champlain
(1567–1635)

Samuel de Champlain

If Jacques Cartier opened the door for the French to the territory of Canada (see no. 4), **Samuel de Champlain** was the man who led them into that territory and established **New France**, the French colony in North America.

Samuel de Champlain was born at Brouage, along France's coast on the Bay of Biscay, and learned navigation from his sea-captain father. As a young man Samuel joined the French army, but he left the service after several years.

In the early 1600s, King **Henry IV** of France was anxious to gain access to the rumored riches of the New World. He commissioned an expedition to go to Canada to establish a fur trade with the Native Americans. In 1603, Champlain traveled to Canada and explored the **St. Lawrence River**

up to the rapids at Lachine, just beyond **Montreal**. Champlain returned in 1604, and this time he started a colony at the mouth of the **St. Croix River** on the Bay of Fundy. In 1605 he moved the colony across the bay to Port Royal (now Annapolis Royal), in Nova Scotia.

During the next three years Champlain explored the coast of North America from Maine to Martha's Vineyard. He discovered most of the major rivers and made the best charts of the coast. In 1608, Champlain started a new colony at the site of **Quebec**, founding the city there. In 1609, he led his French forces along with a war party of Huron Indians that moved against the **Iroquois** to the south; on this expedition, he became the first European to discover the lake that now bears his name. In 1612, Champlain returned to France and received a new grant and a monopoly over the fur trade. He returned to Quebec in 1613 and over the next two years he explored the lands to the west, traveling all the way to Lake Huron and Lake Ontario.

During the winter of 1628 -1629, while France was at war with England, Champlain and the other French settlers at Quebec were cut off from their food supplies by the English. In July 1629, Champlain surrendered to the English; he and about 100 of his men were taken to England. Champlain was held captive there for about a year, and he used his time to write an account of his explorations. The war ended with a treaty in 1632; Chaplain was allowed to return to Quebec the next year, and he died there in 1635.

Having established the permanent settlements that would gradually grow into the country of Canada, Samuel de Champlain earned his reputation as the Father of New France.

15. William Brewster
(1567–1643)

One of the principal leaders of the English colony at Plymouth, **William Brewster** was also one of the few Pilgrims who gave up a position of power and privilege in England to take up the difficult and unknown challenges in the New World.

Brewster's birthplace is unknown, but he was probably born near Scrooby, in north-central England. His father was an important official on the estate of the powerful Archbishop of York, and then became the postmaster on an important stagecoach route. Young William went off to college at Cambridge, but did not stay long enough to earn a degree. Instead, he joined the staff of William Davison, an important official of Queen **Elizabeth I**. From 1585-1586, Brewster accompanied Davison on diplomatic missions to the Netherlands. When Brewster learned of his father's illness in 1589, he returned to Scrooby to serve as his assistant; at his father's death in 1590, Brewster took over both of his positions.

Meanwhile, Brewster had become a member of a Protestant-Puritan congregation that gathered in Scrooby. This group declared themselves "**Separatists**" from the original Puritans, taking a more extreme view of the need to eliminate anything that resembled the practices of the Roman Catholic Church.

Brewster and his companions were persecuted, so in 1608 they went to **Holland**. Although he was never ordained as a minister, Brewster became one of the spiritual leaders of the congregation. To support himself and his growing family, he printed religious books for his fellow Puritans in England. In 1618, one of his books so offended King **James I** of England that the English government pressured the Dutch to force Brewster to shut down his press.

Brewster returned to England and joined with those planning to emigrate to the New World. He sailed on the *Mayflower*, survived the first terrible winter, and became one of the principal leaders of the new congregation in **Plymouth**. Although he had no official religious title, he played a major role in establishing doctrine and procedures for the Plymouth church. He was also active in administering the colony's worldly affairs, and in 1627 he became one of the **Pilgrims** who bought out the interests of the colony's financial supporters.

Brewster prospered in the years that followed. He acquired a fair amount of land, cattle, and other possessions. Governor **William Bradford**, in his history of the Plymouth colony, described Brewster as "of a very cheerful spirit, very sociable and pleasant amongst his friends." It was people like William Brewster—hardy, reliable, dedicated, sincere—who provided the solid foundation for the English colonies in North America.

The Mayflower in Plymouth harbor

16. John Smith
(1579–1631)

Of all the heroic individuals and legendary activities associated with the colonization of North America, Captain **John Smith** and his deeds probably remain among the most popular. Yet most Americans know very little about the actual story of his life.

Born in Lincolnshire County in England, Smith had only a grammar school education before he became apprenticed to a merchant. He left that job around 1596 to seek adventure as a mercenary soldier and fought in several wars. Later he wrote a stirring autobiography of his adventures in Turkey and the Mediterranean Sea.

Smith returned to England around 1604. In 1606 he joined the party of English who were to establish the colony at **Jamestown**. Arriving at Jamestown in April 1607, Smith soon proved himself to be an energetic and adept leader during the struggles the settlers' faced in the early months. In December that year he was taken prisoner by the natives.

According to his own account, Smith was sentenced to die by Chief **Powhatan**. At the last moment, the chief's young daughter **Pocahontas** (see no. 30) begged for Smith's life and he was spared. (There is no other historical evidence to validate this story.)

By September 1608, Smith had assumed effective leadership of the colony, and he organized the desperate colonists to build the necessary structures and to provide food for themselves. When the gentlemen of the colony refused to help build a palisade wall to protect the colony, Smith instituted a new rule: "He that does not work, neither shall he eat." Needless to say, Smith soon found that all hands were ready to contribute.

Smith also explored the nearby coast and created valuable maps. There were constant rivalries within the colony, and after 1609 Smith's powers were somewhat restricted. Then in September 1610 he was wounded in

John Smith

an accidental gunpowder explosion and was forced to return to England to seek proper treatment.

Although Smith never returned to Virginia, he did not abandon his interest in the New World. In 1614 he sailed to North America to search for gold. He sailed the Atlantic coast from Maine to Cape Cod, and although he found no gold, he did return with fish and furs. He also published a map that would prove invaluable to the **Pilgrims** who settled in New England in 1620. Smith made two more attempts to sail to North America in 1615, but was unsuccessful both times.

Smith spent the rest of his years publishing his books and maps. Undoubtedly, many of his stories were exaggerated, but he made North America more accessible to colonizers, and gave future generations of Americans a romantic legend that would live forever.

17. Squanto
(c. 1580–1622)

Squanto, also known as *Tisquantum*, was one of the most-traveled Native Americans of the colonial period. In fact, he probably saw more of the world than most European traders.

Squanto, who was born around 1580, lived in the village of Patuxet on the coast of what is now Massachusetts. Samuel de Champlain visited the harbor at Paxuet in 1605, as did Captain John Smith in 1614.

After Smith departed, Squanto and about 20 of his fellow **Wampanoag Indians** were seized by English Captain Thomas Hunt. Herded on board Hunt's ship, the Wampanoags were taken to Malaga, Spain, where most of them were sold into slavery.

Squanto

Squanto escaped this fate—possibly because of the intervention of some Spanish friars—and eventually made his way to England where he found work. While there, he learned to speak English, which was to be very helpful to him in the future.

Squanto's knowledge of the Atlantic coast was valuable to potential English colonists, and in 1617 he went to Newfoundland to act as a guide. Returning to England, Squanto then shipped out with Captain **Thomas Dermer** in 1619, headed for the New England coast.

Squanto arrived in a land that had been devastated by diseases brought by Europeans. His entire village of Patuxet was empty — all the inhabitants had either died or moved away. When Captain Dermer was wounded in a fight with Native Americans in the waters off Cape Cod, Squanto escaped from the scene, and then settled among the Wampanoags.

English colonists arrived at Patuxet in December 1620 and began to establish **Plymouth Plantation**. In March 1621, Squanto and another Native American, **Samoset**, became the first Indians to meet and speak with the newcomers. Squanto soon emerged as the primary intermediary and interpreter between the Wampanoags, led by **Massasoit**, and the Pilgrims, led by **William Bradford** and **Edward Winslow**.

On the positive side, Squanto showed the Pilgrims the techniques of local agriculture for their crops. On the negative side , Squanto began to accumulate power for himself by playing the Wampanoags and Pilgrims against one another. Furious over Squanto's double-dealing, Massasoit tried to capture him, but the Pilgrims protected their interpreter who had become one of their life lines in the New World. Squanto died from a fever at Plymouth in 1622.

Peter Minuit

Peter Minuit was born in Wesel, at the time part of the German Duchy of Cleves, near the border with Holland. In 1625 he sailed for the new Dutch colony of **New Netherland**, which was sponsored by the privately held West India Company. Whatever status in life Minuit had reached, he was prominent enough to be listed as a member of the Director's Council.

The head of the colony at that time was **Willem Verhulst**, but in September 1626 he was dismissed and sent back to Holland. Minuit was named his successor, and he was officially appointed director-general. It was in this capacity that he "purchased" **Manhattan** from the local Indians. He is said to have paid the Indians with trinkets worth about $24 at that time; certainly their value would be far more in today's money, but still it was a bargain. In any case, the natives did not regard it as a sale, but simply a rent to allow the Dutch to use the land.

Minuit constructed a solid fort on the island and made it the center of the settlement he called **New Amsterdam**. He then worked to bring all the nearby Dutch settlements under the control of his colony. In 1627 he sent representatives to Governor Bradford and the **Plymouth** colony and began trading with the English there.

Meanwhile, Minuit had become engaged in a quarrel with the leaders of the colony's powerful Dutch Reformed Church. In 1631, the Amsterdam authorities of the West India Company recalled Minuit to Holland. After a hearing, they dismissed him. Minuit retired to the place of his youth, the Duchy of Cleves.

In 1637, the Swedish government decided to sponsor a Swedish trading colony on the **Delaware River**. A former director of the West India Company who admired Minuit recommended him as the right man to head such an enterprise. Minuit agreed, and he even invested a large sum of his own money in the undertaking. He sailed in the fall of 1637, and in March 1638 purchased a large tract of land on the Delaware River. The settlement was named **New Sweden**, and Minuit directed the building of Fort Christina, on the site of modern-day **Wilmington**, Delaware. When the trading post was completed, Minuit sailed for the Caribbean island of St. Christopher, where he exchanged his cargo for tobacco. While he was visiting another Dutch ship there, a hurricane struck and he was lost at sea.

Minuit was a hard-working and hard-driving—and perhaps even hard-headed—businessman. Men like him made valuable contributions to establishing colonies in North America. The settlement Minuit founded at New Amsterdam would eventually be renamed **New York City**.

19. Miles Standish
(c. 1584–1656)

Miles Standish

Miles Standish was born in Lancashire county in northwest England, and his family was evidently Roman Catholic. Not much else is known of his early years except that he served in the Netherlands and Belgium as a mercenary soldier. Because of his reputation as a military man, he was hired by the **Pilgrim** colonists to go along when they sailed to North America in 1620.

After landing at Plymouth, the Pilgrims came to rely greatly on Standish's practical experience. Over the first winter, he was one of only a handful of colonists who did not become terribly ill, and he helped to nurse the others. He also became adept at dealing with the local tribes, even learning their dialects. Standish designed and supervised the construction of the Plymouth's fort, and he organized various other measures to defend the colony.

By 1625, the **Plymouth Colony** was having financial and legal problems with its sponsors in England. Standish was asked to return home to negotiate on behalf of the colony. He went to England, and although he did not have much success in negotiations, he returned in 1626 with some loans and valuable supplies. In 1627 he became one of the financial supporters of the colony, and from that point on he held several important positions within the colony's administration. In 1628 he also led the expedition from Plymouth that broke up the unruly Merry Mount settlement in nearby Quincy, led by the renegade **Thomas Morton**.

Standish's first wife had died during the first winter, and in 1624 he married a woman who had come over from England the previous year. More than 200 years later, **Henry Wadsworth Longfellow** wrote his well-known poem—*The Courtship of Miles Standish*. The poem tells of how Standish, too shy to ask **Priscilla Mullins** to marry him, asks fellow colonist **John Alden** to propose on his behalf. In fact, Alden also loves Priscilla, and when he proposes for Standish, Priscilla asked, "Why don't you speak for yourself, John?" Although Longfellow's poem is one of the most beloved and oft-quoted poems in American literature, there is no basis for the tale.

In fact, Alden—who did indeed marry Priscilla —and Standish were friends. In 1631 they founded the adjacent town of Duxbury, where Standish lived during his later years.

Standish was a striking man, short, rather stout, and with a florid complexion and red hair. His enemy, Thomas Morton, called him "Captain Shrimp," and another acquaintance described him as follows: "A little chimney soon fired." However, no description ever denied that Standish was a brave, hardy, and irreplaceable member of New England's first colony.

Americans might be forgiven for thinking that **John Rolfe** is a fictional character. His name is associated with some of the more legendary stories in colonial history, including the events that served as a basis for Shakespeare's *The Tempest*, the legends about Pocahontas, and the raising of tobacco.

As with so many of the first colonists, information about Rolfe's early years is sketchy. He was born in Norfolk County on the east-central coast of England and was married around 1608. In 1609 he set off with his wife for the colony at **Jamestown** on the ship commanded by Christopher Newport. Late in September, the ship was wrecked in the Bermudas and the voyagers were stranded on an island there. His wife soon gave birth to their daughter, who died shortly thereafter. The shipwrecked survivors constructed two small boats and sailed for Virginia, arriving at Jamestown in May, 1610. Shakespeare based his final play, *The Tempest*, on an account of the shipwreck.

Once settled at Jamestown, Rolfe was attracted to the tobacco that the Indians grew and smoked. Some Englishmen had tried smoking it, but most people found it harsh and unpleasant. Around 1612 Rolfe began experimenting with new ways of cultivating and curing tobacco, and before long the tobacco crop became the basis of the Virginia colony's economy.

Rolfe's wife had died shortly after arriving in Virginia. In 1613, the English settlers took **Pocahontas**—the daughter of the great chief **Powhatan**—hostage in revenge for the Indians holding several colonists as prisoners. Rolfe and Pocahontas fell in love. She converted to **Christianity**, adopted the name Rebecca, and married him. This led to a period of peace between the colonists and the Indians.

Rolfe took Pocahontas to England in 1616 where she was treated as a celebrity. However, while preparing to return to Virginia, she became ill with smallpox and died in 1617. She had one son, Thomas, who was educated in England, and who went to Virginia and continued the family line that many later Virginians were proud to claim.

Rolfe himself returned to Virginia in 1617, where he prospered in the tobacco trade. He also married for a third time. He served as secretary and recorder of the colony until 1619, and in 1621 he was appointed to the Council of State.

In 1622, Rolfe was killed in the Indian attack led by Powhatan's brother and successor, **Opechancanough**. Ironically, the success of the tobacco crops had ensured the permanence of the English colony. The need for more land drove the growers to expand deeper and deeper into Indian lands, and this in turn led the natives to their desperate revolt.

John Rolfe marries Pocahontas

Thomas Hooker
(c. 1586–1647)

Thomas Hooker giving a sermon

One of the greatest of the Puritan ministers, **Thomas Hooker** was born in Marfield, Leicestershire, England, around 1586. After earning his bachelor's and master's degrees at Cambridge, he became an Anglican minister and was appointed the rector of Esher, Surrey, in 1620. Hooker soon became an important **Puritan** leader. He married Susan Garbrand in 1621 and the couple had three children.

When Hooker's Puritan leanings were fully confirmed, he attracted the displeasure of Anglican Archbishop William Laud. Hooker was forced to leave his post at Esher, so he opened a school at Little Baddow, where **John Eliot** (see no. 37) served as his assistant. Fearing further persecution, Hooker fled to the Netherlands in 1630. Pondering his options, he considered migrating to Barbados, but decided on New England instead. He left Holland, returned briefly to England, and then sailed for Boston, where he arrived on September 4, 1633, in the company of Reverend John Cotton and Samuel Stone. The Puritans in Boston were delighted. They declared they now had "Cotton for their clothing, Hooker for their fishing, and Stone for their building."

Hooker became the Puritan pastor at Newtown, just west of Boston. He found his flock there restless and eager to venture beyond the narrow strip of coastal settlements. Heeding their desire, in 1636 he led the congregation on a migratory move from Newtown to what is now **Hartford**, Connecticut. (The move was illustrated in a famous 19th century painting by Frederick Church.)

Firmly settled at Hartford, Hooker became his own man. Unlike **John Winthrop** (see no. 22), Hooker was a born democrat. He believed the Congregational Church of New England provided an ideal model for both church and civil government. He preached a famous sermon before the General Court of Connecticut in which he trumpeted the sacredness of the "free consent of the people." When Connecticut accepted the Fundamental Orders of 1639 as its first constitution, Hooker's democratic ideas were firmly incorporated within the document.

Hooker died at Hartford in 1647, having left his intellectual mark on the Connecticut colony. His most important written work, *A Survey of the Summe of Church Discipline*, published a year after his death, is one of the clearest expositions of the congregational system ever produced. One irony of Hooker's life was his feud with **William Pynchon**, the powerful colonist, trader, and land speculator from the northern settlement of **Springfield**. In 1638, Pynchon severed relations with Hooker and Hartford, and he connected Springfield to the administration of Massachusetts. Had the two men seen eye to eye, it is possible that western Massachusetts and Connecticut—linked by their common dependence on the Connecticut River—would have become one colony, and later one state.

22. John Winthrop
(1587–1649)

The first governor of the Massachusetts Bay colony, **John Winthrop** was born at Edwardstone, England, in 1587. Winthrop was educated at Cambridge University, and practiced law in London from 1613-1629. By this time he was financially secure, and his religious faith had shifted to a complete acceptance of the **Puritan** faith, so he sought a way to worship in greater freedom. When a group of middle-class Puritans laid the groundwork to create a colony in New England, Winthrop cast his lot with them.

Winthrop was a natural leader, and he soon took on the executive work of the group. In 1629—even before they left England—the colonists chose him to be governor of the new colony of **Massachusetts Bay**.

Winthrop and his family sailed on board the *Arbella* from Southampton, England on March 22, 1630. They reached Salem, Massachusetts, on June 12 and began at once to establish the colony. Winthrop was instrumental in carrying out the move to a peninsula that the Native Americans called "Shawmut," which soon became known as **Boston**.

Due to his legal training and great commitment to the Puritan cause, Winthrop remained the most important leader in Boston for the rest of his life. He served as governor of the colony on several different occasions—from 1629-1634, 1637 -1640, 1642 -1644, and 1646 -1649. Winthrop believed in the rule of the "godly elect," those whose lives and fortunes reflected sobriety, piety, and service to the community. He was no early type of democrat; Winthrop remained a lifetime believer in class distinctions.

Winthrop was deputy governor when the religious case involving **Anne Marbury Hutchinson** (see no. 26) came to trial in 1637. He read the "guilty" sentence to Hutchinson. When she asked for amplification of the court's reasons, he responded: "Say no more, the court knows wherefore and is satisfied."

In 1643, Winthrop was also influential in bringing together a number of colonists under the auspices of the United Colonies of New England. One of his dearest hopes was that Puritanism would spread throughout all of New England, but in this he was disappointed. The **Quaker** colony in **Rhode Island** and a number of small dissident communities outlasted both Winthrop and his generation of Puritans.

His book, *A Journal of the Transactions and Occurrences in the Settlement of Massachusetts... 1630 to 1644*, published in 1790, is a moving testament to the sincerity of his beliefs and his elegant social graces.

John Winthrop

23. William Claiborne
(c. 1587–1677)

William Claiborne

The second son of the lord of the manor of Cleburne, **William Claiborne** was born in Westmoreland County, England, around 1587. Little is known of his early years in England. He first appeared in America in 1622, as the surveyor of the Virginia colony. Claiborne prospered in his work and rose steadily in the colonial bureaucracy; eventually King **Charles I** appointed him treasurer of the colony in 1642. Claiborne, however, was ambitious to begin a colony of his own.

Claiborne firmly opposed the founding of the Maryland colony by **Leonard Calvert** (see no. 39). Claiborne set up a trading post on Kent Island in **Chesapeake Bay**, squarely in between the Virginia colony and the newly designated Catholic colony in Maryland. He had purchased the island from the local native tribe, and began a brisk trade with them in corn and tobacco. The island prospered so much that a resident was sent to Virginia to represent the island in the House of Burgesses. Claiborne, however, soon ran afoul of the Calvert family.

Learning that Claiborne was inciting the Native Americans of the Chesapeake region against the Catholics in Maryland, the colony's proprietor, **Cecilius Calvert**, ordered his brother, Leonard, the governor, to arrest Claiborne. The governor was unable to accomplish this, since Claiborne went to England on his own accord in 1637. The Maryland governor took over the jurisdiction of Kent Island during Claiborne's absence.

Meanwhile, the legal case finally came to a head in England. The Commission of Plantations found in favor of the Calvert family in their suits against Claiborne, and it appeared as if Claiborne had finally been defeated.

However, in October 1644, Claiborne and English sea captain **Richard Ingle** carried out a full-scale rebellion against the Calvert family. Claiborne, Ingle, and their forces drove Governor Calvert into Virginia, and gained control of the Maryland province, which they held until December, 1646.

In 1651, Claiborne was appointed to a commission of the **Puritan Parliament** that governed the plantations of the Chesapeake Bay region. The affairs of the Maryland colony were under the control of this body from 1652 until 1657, and Claiborne used all his skill to thwart the wishes of the Calverts.

Claiborne was forced to relinquish his authority in Maryland after King Charles II was restored to the English throne in 1660. Claiborne even lost control of Kent Island. Toward the end of his long life, Claiborne sent one last petition to King **Charles II**, asking that Kent Island be restored to him. His request was refused, but Claiborne retained his reputation as one of the feistiest and most contentious of all leaders in colonial North America.

24. John Endicott
(1589-1665)

Historians use adjectives such as bigoted, zealous, courageous, honest and high-tempered to describe **John Endicott**. A colonial governor of **Massachusetts** and strong Puritan leader, Endicott has also been singled-out as being responsible for instigating the **Pequot War**.

Endicott was born in Devonshire, England to wealthy parents; his parents disowned their son when he became associated with the Reverends **John White** and **Samuel Skelton** and joined the Puritan movement. In 1628, along with his wife, Endicott led a small group of emigrants from England to Naumkeag, modern-day Salem, Massachusetts. Endicott served as acting-governor for two years until **John Winthrop** arrived in 1630. Endicott remained in Salem while Winthrop went on to establish the town of Boston.

John Endicott

A strict Puritan, Endicott organized his own church on the model of the **Pilgrims** at Plymouth, and ran his colony sternly. He hated Quakers and treated them very harshly. He forced women to wear veils at public assemblies, was opposed to long hair, and did not allow the cultivation of tobacco.

In 1636, the Standing Council responsible for military matters, sent Endicott to lead an expedition to punish the Block Island and **Pequot Indians**; the Block Island Indians were held responsible for the death of a trader, John Oldham. Governor Henry Vane gave Endicott instructions to take possession of the island, kill all the men, and take the women and children as slaves. Upon landing, Endicott's forces were unable to find most of the Island's inhabitants and decided to burn and pillage the empty villages.

Endicott was also instructed to sail to Pequot territory and demand payment from them as well as the warriors responsible for the murder of a Virginian named John Stone, who had been killed three years earlier. After meeting with a Pequot ambassador, Endicott could not be appeased and ordered his men to attack. As with the assault on Block Island , Endicott's forces could not find warriors to engage in battle and resorted to destroying Pequot villages. Endicott then returned to Massachusetts Bay, without meeting either of his objectives.

However, his attack had outraged the Pequots. They responded with a guerrilla campaign against English settlers in **Connecticut** that erupted into the Pequot War. The war lasted a year, and when it ended the Puritans had established themselves as a major force in New England and ended the dominance of the Pequot tribe.

Endicott served on-and-off as deputy governor and governor of the Massachusetts colony from 1641 to 1665. He died in Boston on March 15, 1665.

Signing of the Mayflower Compact

William Bradford came from humble beginnings. He was born to a farming family in Austerfield, Yorkshire, England. Trained from an early age to follow the family occupation, he nonetheless displayed a great love of learning, and he joined the small group of Dissenters from the Anglican Church that met at the home of **William Brewster** (see no. 15) in Scrooby. In 1609, Bradford went with the **Separatists** to Amsterdam and then to Leyden, both in the United Provinces of the Netherlands.

Eleven years in the Netherlands convinced Bradford and his fellows that they did not want their children to grow up more Dutch than English. Therefore, they went back to England and chartered two ships, the *Mayflower* and the *Speedwell*, to take them to the New World. The *Speedwell* proved to be unseaworthy, so the *Mayflower* sailed alone from England on September 6, 1620. On Novemebr 10, it arrived off Cape Cod, and the next day forty-one of the adult male passengers signed the **Mayflower Compact**; Bradford was the second to sign, after John Carver.

Bradford's common sense and grave sense of duty won him great respect among his fellow Pilgrims, and in April, 1621 he was elected the first governor of the new colony.

Bradford was at this time struggling to overcome personal grief. His wife, **Dorothy May**, whom he had married in Amsterdam in 1613, had drowned in Cape Cod harbor in 1620. He married **Alice Southworth** in 1623 and together the couple had three children.

Although he came from simple origins, Bradford was no democrat. He thought it necessary and proper that an elite should govern the new colony. Devout by nature, Bradford began to see the hand of God in all the things that helped the Pilgrim colonists survive. In his diary, which was later published as *History of Plimoth Plantation* (1620-1647), Bradford time and again referred to the hand of Providence operating on behalf of the **Pilgrims**. Thus, the appearance of **Samoset** and **Squanto** (see no. 17) and their subsequent instructions on how to farm and fish, were seen as a favor from of God.

After his first term as governor, Bradford was re-elected 30 times in the next 35 years. He outlived nearly all of the original Pilgrims and remained an icon of virtue to the community. In later years, the writings in his diary exhibited a depressing tone, as he realized the Pilgrims were too small in number to remain pure, and that their community would be absorbed by other, larger communities.

Anne Marbury Hutchinson
(1591–1643)

Anne Marbury was born in Alford, Lincolnshire, England in 1591. Her father and her maternal grandfather were both Anglican priests, and she grew up in a household that was accustomed to religious discussion. The Marburys moved to London in 1605. In 1612, Anne married William Hutchinson, a merchant from Alford, and moved there. The couple had 14 children.

Seeking greater opportunities, the Hutchinson family emigrated to the New World aboard the ship the *Griffin* in 1634. They arrived in Boston and soon became valued members of the Puritan community.

Sometime in 1636, Anne Hutchinson began to hold religious meetings with women at her home at which the group discussed such issues as the minister's latest Sunday sermon. Although the meetings began as informal affairs, Anne soon began to speak of a "covenant of grace" rather than the "covenant of works" accepted in Puritan circles. This meant that she believed that God's grace was large enough to allow each human being to make his or her own peace with God, rather than having to rely upon the intercession of a minister or priest.

She was not rejected at first. John Cotton, one of the most important Puritan ministers, initially agreed with her, and she was protected through the good will of other political leaders, such as Henry Vane. However, after Vane left the colony in 1637, she came under attack and was eventually charged with Antinomianism—the heretical belief that ministers and the established church were unnecessary.

A meeting of the Puritan churches was held in 1637, and the matter was sent for deliberation to the General Court, the legislature of the Massachusetts Bay Colony. Hutchinson was found guilty and sentenced to banishment from the colony. After

Governor John Winthrop read the sentence, Hutchinson asked for the reasons why she had been found guilty. Winthrop gave the frosty reply that it was sufficient for only the court to know the reasons for her banishment.

In 1638, Hutchinson, her family, and a large number of her associates migrated to Aquidneck, in what would soon become Rhode Island. Her husband died in 1642 and Hutchinson and some of her children then moved to Pelham Bay on Long Island. They were surprised by an Indian attack in August, 1643, and Hutchinson and all but one of the children with her were killed in the raid. Some Puritan leaders saw this as proof that God had indeed been displeased by her conduct.

A statue to Anne Hutchinson—as a fighter for religious freedom—stands today on the Boston Common in the center of Boston.

Anne Marbury Hutchinson

Johan Björnsson Printz—the "**Lion of New Sweden**"—was born in Bottnaryd, Smaland, Sweden, in 1592. As a young man, Printz studied theology in Germany and seemed destined for the ministry. However, he was seized by a group of roving soldiers in Germany who forced him to join their ranks, and he went to Italy as a mercenary soldier.

The change fitted Printz surprisingly well. He served as a mercenary for Austria and Denmark; while serving in that capacity for the German state of Brunswick, Printz met and married **Elizabeth von Boche**, the daughter of an important Brunswick official. Printz joined the Swedish army in 1625 and rose to the rank of lieutenant colonel. His wife died around 1640, and he married Maria von Linnestau in 1642. In April of that same year he was named director, or governor, of **New Sweden**, a fledgling colony set up on the banks of the **Delaware River**. He was knighted by Queen Christina and sailed for the New World in 1643.

Johan Printz

Printz served as governor for slightly more than 10 years. A man of tremendous appetite, he grew to nearly 400 pounds and was known as "Big Guts" by the Native Americans in the region. Despite his physical size, Printz was active and energetic. He built a blockhouse, a church, a wharf, a grist mill, and a brewery. Printz greatly encouraged trade, and New Sweden became known for its two major exports: tobacco and beaver skins.

Printz was clearly out to make his fortune as well as to enlarge the possessions of Queen Christina. He had a house built for himself on Tinicum Island and called it New Gothenborg. Printz also owned a pleasure yacht, the first of its type in North America.

Although he made peace with the Indians, and gave land to farmers, Printz could be a severe leader. In 1653 a group of settlers asked permission to send a petition to Sweden to request mediation in a dispute between the governor and the populace. To Printz, this was clearly treason. He had **Anders Jonsson**, one of the group's leaders, executed at once. A few months later, however, Printz decided that trying to govern the tiny colony without the real support of its inhabitants was impossible. He handed over the government to his deputy, **Johan Papegoja**, and sailed for home.

Printz later became commander of Jonkoping Castle and then governor of his own native district of Jonkoping Lan. He died after a fall from his horse in 1663.

28. Jean de Brébeuf
(1593–1649)

Best known as one of the eight "North American Martyrs," **Jean de Brébeuf** was born at Conde-sur-Vire in Normandy, France in 1593. He entered the **Jesuit** order in 1617 and was ordained a priest at Rouen in 1622. Three years later, his order sent him to the struggling colony of New France to win converts to the Catholic faith.

Brébeuf arrived at **Quebec** and spent five months with the **Montagnais Indians**, learning their language. In 1626, he embarked on an 800-mile canoe trip to the Huron country— in what is now **Ontario**—where he chose to live with the Bear Tribe. While he was there, he translated the teachings of the Catholic church into the Huron language.

Brébeuf returned to Quebec and then spent time in France before he traveled with three companions to live again among the **Hurons**. His work was difficult and slow. The first adult Huron to convert did so in 1637, and four years later there was still only a total of 60 converts among the tribe.

Brébeuf's worst years among the Indians came in 1636 and 1637 when the Huron were struck by sickness. The Hurons turned against Brébeuf for a time, but he managed to win their trust yet again. After he suffered a bad fall on the ice, Brébeuf returned to Quebec where he managed another Indian mission at the town of Sillery. However, his heart was still closest to the mission that was farthest away, that of the Huron. Therefore he returned to their country in 1644 and renewed his work among them.

Brébeuf's return coincided with the start of a war between the Huron and the people of the **Five Nations of Iroquois**. The war was sparked by rivalry over the beaver trade, and the Iroquois launched ferocious assaults on the Huron towns. Brébeuf and his fellow missionaries found themselves caught in the middle of this struggle. Brébeuf felt the Huron were his spiritual charges and he could not abandon them in the time of their greatest need.

On March 16, 1649, Brébeuf and Father **Gabriel Lalement** left Fort St. Marie at Midland in modern-day Ontario. They were seized by Iroquois and brought to St. Ignace where the two men were tortured and put to death. The Huron mission died with Brébeuf, but the scattered Huron who escaped from the Iroquois turned in greater numbers to the Catholic faith.

Brébeuf, Lalement, and six other priests were named saints in 1930. Known as the "North American Martyrs," these men were recognized in 1940 as the patron saints of Canada.

Jean de Brébeuf

Port Royal

One of the most colorful colonial leaders, **Charles Saint-Étienne de La Tour** was born in Champagne, France. His father, Claude de Saint-Étienne de La Tour brought him from France to **Acadia** (modern-day Nova Scotia) in 1610.

The La Tours built up Port Royal (modern-day Annapolis Royal) but the English buccaneer **Samuel Argall** looted the town in 1613. Undeterred, the La Tours rebuilt. When Charles de Biencourt, leader of the settlement died in 1623, he named Charles La Tour as his heir.

Charles then built Fort Lomeron at **Cape de Sable**. In 1627, England and France went to war and suddenly all the French possessions in the New World were at risk. When Charles' father Claude was captured by the English while at sea, he pledged himself to the English cause and sailed against the very fort his son had built. Charles fought off the attack by his father's troops and held Fort Lomeron. When the war ended, King **Louis XIII** made Isaac de Razilly governor of all of Acadia. De Razilly in turn named Charles La Tour and **Charles de Menou d'Aulnay** as his top lieutenants—La Tour to be given the territory east of the **St. Croix River**, and d'Aulnay the portion west of it. La Tour and d'Aulnay—both ambitious, energetic, and competitive—were soon at odds.

From 1647 until 1657 the two men fought an on-again, off-again war. While La Tour held the fort, his courageous wife **Francoise-Marie Jacquelin** went to France in 1642. She won the court over to her husband's cause and returned with supply ships. Finding La Tour blockaded at Fort Sainte-Marie by d'Aulnay's ships, she and her husband asked help from the **Puritans** in Boston; with their assistance, they were able to break the blockade.

Since La Tour had won his assistance from English colonists, D'Aulnay won favor in France and was given command of Acadia. He captured La Tour's fort in 1646; Madame La Tour was killed in the fighting. Only after d'Aulnay died in 1650, was La Tour able to reestablish himself in the good graces of the French court.

La Tour brought new colonists to Acadia in 1653. Determined to put the past behind him, he courted and then married **Jeanne Motin**, d'Aulnay's widow!

In 1654, after English Major **Robert Sedgwick** captured Saint-Marie and La Tour was taken as a prisoner to England. He remained there until 1656, when he accepted English conditions for his return. La Tour was to act as an agent for the English government, and in return, he would be allowed to assume his old estates in Acadia. La Tour then went into retirement at Cape de Sable.

30. Pocahontas
(c. 1595–1617)

Pocahontas was born on the western side of Chesapeake Bay in modern-day Virginia around 1595. Her father was **Powhatan**, chief of the Renape tribe of **Algonquin Indians**. Her life, and that of thousands of her people, was changed dramatically by the appearance of a group of English colonists in 1607. Initially, the settlers occupied only a small peninsula of land they called **Jamestown**, but as they began to expand to the north and west, they encroached on Powhatan's territory.

The first record in English documents regarding Pocahontas came from English Captain **John Smith** (see no. 16) who claimed that the Indian princess saved him from death at the hands of Powhatan's men. According to Smith, he was thrown to the ground and was about to be beheaded when Pocahontas threw herself between Smith and his captors, and begged her father to save the Englishman's life.

Pocahontas

The story has been debated by historians ever since. Some assert that John Smith was a glory seeker who would do and say anything to enhance his reputation; other historians see no reason the story should be rejected.

What is certain is that Smith returned to Jamestown from his captivity and that Pocahontas began to serve as a go-between between the English and Native Americans. Her contact with John Smith was broken late in 1609 when he returned to England because of an injury caused by a gunpowder explosion.

In December 1612, the English captain **Samuel Argall** kidnaped Pocahontas and held her as a hostage at Jamestown. While she was being held, Pocahontas was converted to Christianity by Reverend **Alexander Whitaker**. She took the Christian name Rebecca.

John Rolfe (see no. 20), an English adventurer, met and fell in love with Rebecca. Rolfe asked the colony's Governor, Thomas Dale, for approval of their marriage. Dale agreed, believing that the marriage would help relations between the Indians and the English colonists. The wedding took place in April, 1614. A fragile peace ensued between the Indians and English, during which the English colony continued to grow.

In 1616, John Rolfe, Rebecca, and their infant son Thomas went to England. In London, the "Lady Rebecca" was brought before King **James I** and his queen; the monarchs and London society were greatly impressed by her manner and appearance. The Rolfes intended to return to Virginia in 1617, but Pocahontas fell ill and died before they left. Her husband and son returned to Virginia, and eventually Thomas Rolfe became a member of the Tidewater aristocracy. Through him, Pocahontas's blood descended to numerous generations of Americans. The 28th president of the United States, **Woodrow Wilson**, was one of her descendants.

Edward Winslow

Edward Winslow was born at Droitwitch, Worcestershire, England in 1595. An early convert to the **Puritan** cause, he moved to the Netherlands, where he married Elizabeth Barker in 1618.

Winslow and his wife sailed on the Mayflower, bound for the New World, in 1620. Upon their arrival at **Plymouth**, Winslow rose to a place of leadership in the new colony. In 1621, he negotiated the first treaty between the **Pilgrims** and the Native American leader, Chief **Massasoit**. Aside from **Miles Standish** (see no. 19), Winslow was the Pilgrim who carried the most influence with the neighboring Indian tribes.

Following the death of his wife, Winslow married Susanna White, the widowed mother of Peregrine White, the first English child born in the northern colonies. The marriage between Winslow and White was the settlers' first marriage conducted in New England.

Because of his diplomatic skill, Winslow was sent to England twice to represent the colony. While there in 1624, he published *Good Newes from New England: or a True Relation of Things Very Remarkable at the Plantation of Plimoth*. This book was important in bringing the colony to the minds of thousands of potential English immigrants.

In 1629, Winslow became the official agent for the colony, and continued to make many visits to his native country. On one of his trips in 1635, he was imprisoned for four months on the order of Archbishop William Laud, who deplored the Pilgrims' approach to church doctrine.

While in New England, Winslow became active in trade with the Native Americans. He set up trading posts on the coast of Maine, and intended to extend his activities to the south as well. Public duties called, however, and he served as governor of the Plymouth colony in 1633, 1636 and 1644.

In 1646, Winslow returned to England on another visit. This time he was caught up in the turmoil of the English Civil War and was unable to return to Plymouth. He rejoiced at the victory of the Puritan forces, which brought the end of the monarchy, and the institution of the Commonwealth government under **Oliver Cromwell**, who became Lord Protector of England. Cromwell honored Winslow with several appointments, and in 1649, Winslow became a founding member of the Society for the Propagation of the Gospel.

Winslow died from fever while he was on a campaign with English forces in an attempt to capture Jamaica in the West Indies. He was buried at sea. Winslow was the only Pilgrim leader whose appearance was recorded in a portrait, which was painted in London in 1651.

32. Lion Gardiner
(1599–1663)

One of the most unlikely of the colonial leaders, was Englishman **Lion Gardiner**. Born in England in 1599, Gardiner's activities first date from 1635, when he was a military engineer serving with the Dutch army in the Netherlands. There he became acquainted with Puritan ministers such as John Davenport, who was later one of the founders of New Haven, Connecticut.

That same year, several English Lords planned to establish a new colony at the mouth of the Connecticut River. (The town of **Saybrook** still stands there today.) The noblemen hired Gardiner to go to the New World as an engineer, and build a fort at the river's mouth. In return, he was to receive free transportation for his family, and 100 pounds sterling per year.

Pequot Indians

Gardiner and his wife Mary arrived in Boston late in 1635. Gardiner built a fort at the harbor's entrance that winter, and in the spring he and his wife journeyed southwest to the mouth of the Connecticut River. Gardiner built a fort there, as promised, and his son David and daughter Mary were the first English children born in what is now Connecticut.

When the **Pequot War** broke out in 1637,

Gardiner and his garrison at the fort came under attack. They fended off the assault, but Gardiner complained to the Puritan leader John Endicott that, "You come hither to raise these wasps about my ears, and then you will take wing and fly away." This was true enough; the Pequot Indians could not venture to attack Boston or Plymouth, but they could threaten the safety of Gardiner, his family, and his soldiers.

After Gardiner participated in the campaign that destroyed the Pequots in May, 1637, he looked for a safer location. In 1640, he bought an island off the coast of **Long Island** from the Indians for ten coats of trading cloth. He and his family moved there in 1641.

Although he moved to East Hampton, Long Island in 1653, he was best known as the proprietor of what became known as "**Gardiner's Island.**"

In 1665, after Gardiner's death, New York Governor Nicoll confirmed David Gardiner as heir to the island. In 1686, Governor Thomas Dongan raised the island to the level of an English manor. The Gardiner family still holds the island, which has the distinction of being the oldest surviving manor in North America.

33. Massasoit
(c. 1600–1661)

Known to his own people as Ousamequin ("Yellow Feather"), **Chief Massasoit** was the most influential Native American to welcome the **Pilgrims** when they arrived at Plymouth.

Massasoit was born around 1600 and became chief of the Pokanoket group of **Wampanoag Indians**. When the Pilgrims arrived at Plymouth in 1620, Massasoit sent men to watch the newcomers from a distance. He wanted to know something about these strangers before he met them face to face. Therefore, it was **Samoset,** and then English-speaking **Squanto**, who were the first Native Americans to meet the Pilgrims. Then Massasoit decided to meet the newcomers himself.

On March 22, 1621, Massasoit and 60 warriors arrived at Plymouth. Massasoit met with the Pilgrim leaders and he soon made a treaty of friendship and peace between their two peoples. The pact called for mutual defense in case either people was attacked by a third party.

The final clause read, "That so doing, their sovereign lord, King James, would esteem him as his friend and ally." American historians have long noted that Massasoit kept the treaty for the next 40 years of his life. This is undoubtedly true, but what is often overlooked is the fact that Massasoit felt trapped between two potential enemies: the **Narragansett Indians** to his west and the Pilgrims to the east. Therefore, it was essential for him to be at peace with at least one of those groups.

Massasoit and 90 of his people went to Plymouth to celebrate the first **Thanksgiving** in November, 1621. They brought five deer with them, and the feast confirmed an era of peace and respect between the two peoples.

As the years and decades passed, Massasoit witnessed the arrival of more and more European settlers. Though he left no record of his thoughts on the matter, Massasoit encouraged his people to adapt and use some of the tools and farming methods the settlers brought. The Wampanoags began to use iron hoes; they also began to raise chicken and sheep. By the time of Massasoit's death in 1660, many of his people were practicing skills learned from the Europeans. When the Pilgrims broke the spirit of the 1621 treaty by trying to make the Wampanoags subjects instead of allies, Plymouth and other English settlements faced the last strong effort by the native population to resist their expansion. This effort was led by **Metacomet** (see no. 50), Massasoit's son and heir.

Massasoit and John Carver

34. Margaret Brent
(c. 1601–1671)

The Governor's Castle at St. Mary's City

On January 21, 1648, **Margaret Brent** startled the Maryland Assembly by asking for the right to vote. Margaret felt that she deserved two votes—one because she was a landowner and another because she had been given power by the late Governor Calvert. Some historians believe her to be the first true American feminist; others consider her to be a remarkable businesswoman who was more interested in her own personal advancement than in the advancement of all women.

Brent was born in Gloucester county, England, around 1601. She was one of the 13 children of wealthy Richard Brent. Raised a Roman Catholic, Margaret decided to leave England when she was in her thirties and join the Catholic colony of **Maryland**. In 1638, she, and three of her siblings immigrated to Maryland.

Margaret and her sister Mary Brent received a grant of more than 70 acres in St. Mary's City; the property became known as the "Sisters Freehold." Margaret also acquired 1,000 acres of land on Kent Island in the middle of **Chesapeake Bay**, and she appeared frequently in court to collect debts owed to her.

The Brent family acquired high social status in Maryland after Governor **Leonard**

Calvert (see no. 39) married Anne Brent, another of the Brent sisters. In May 1647, as he lay dying, Calvert named Margaret Brent as his executor, telling her to "Take all, pay all."

Margaret Brent faced a difficult situation. Just prior to his death, Governor Calvert had squelched the Claiborne Rebellion. He had brought soldiers from Virginia to accomplish this, and when he died there was no money to pay the troops. The colony stood on the verge of chaos.

Undaunted, Brent imported corn from Virginia to feed the soldiers. Finding that Governor Calvert's estate was inadequate to pay the men, she gained a power of attorney to act on behalf of **Cecil Calvert**—the late governor's brother, who was Lord Baltimore, the Colony's Proprietor living in England. She then sold his cattle to obtain the money owed the troops. The new governor, Thomas Green, was then able to re-establish order in the province. However, despite her actions in behalf of the colony, when Brent demanded two votes in the Maryland assembly, Governor Green denied her request.

In 1651, Margaret and Mary Brent moved across Chesapeake Bay to the Virginia colony and acquired large tracts of land in **Westmoreland County**. As lady of the manor, Margaret held regular feasts and celebrations for her people, and was generally well loved.

No other woman in colonial America held as much power as Margaret Brent did in 1647 and 1648. The trust shown her by Governor Calvert, and the power he handed her were unique.

Roger Williams was one of the few seekers of religious freedom who was willing to grant that same liberty to people who had beliefs other than his. Williams was born in London, the son of a merchant tailor. He earned his bachelor's degree at Cambridge College in 1627 and took holy orders as an Anglican minister in 1629. In the same year, he married Mary Barnard. Soon, Williams left the church and joined the ranks of the **Separatists** and Puritans—dissidents who came to believe the Anglican church was corrupt and retained too many Catholic practices.

In 1630, Williams and his wife decided to migrate to the Massachusetts Bay Colony, where other Puritans had gone seeking religious freedom. After rejecting a minister's position in Boston, Williams settled in **Plymouth**—founded

Roger Williams

by the Separatists—where his views were more accepted. He established close ties with the Indians in the area, and soon came to believe that—since they preceded the colonists in the New World—England was unjustly giving away charters to English settlers to land it did not own. In addition, Williams' political views held that in order to insure the purity of the church, affairs of the church and state must be totally separate, and that the state must tolerate a variety of religious sects.

Williams' views—both concerning the Indians and the separation of church and state—greatly disturbed the Massachusetts Bay Colony's leaders. His beliefs undermined the basic principles upon which the colony had been founded. The leaders tried to get him to change his views, or to keep them to himself. When he refused, they finally banished him from the colony in 1635.

Cast out, Williams wandered through southeastern Massachusetts. He was welcomed by Chief **Massasoit** (see no. 33) who gave him shelter during the winter of 1635-1636. In April 1636, Williams purchased land from Indians and started the tiny town of **Providence**. Living right in the midst of Wampanoag and Narragansett territory, Williams found it essential to be on good terms with the natives. He learned their language and cultivated friendly relations with the Indian leaders.

Williams wanted to establish a colony in which the people would be free to worship according to their own views. In 1643, he went to England and petitioned King **Charles I** for a charter. Williams's efforts were rewarded in 1644 with a new charter for the Providence territory, which eventually became Rhode Island. In later years, Williams continued to advocate religious liberty and democracy, notably in books he wrote such as, *The Bloody Tenet Yet More Bloody* (1652). He served as Rhode Island's governor from 1654-1657, and remained active in the colony's affairs until his death.

36. Simon Bradstreet & Anne Bradstreet (1603–1697; 1612–1672)

One of the most remarkable husband and wife combinations in Colonial America, the Bradstreets contributed to the Massachusetts Bay Colony in politics, religion, and literature.

Simon Bradstreet was born in Horbling, England in 1603, the son of an Anglican minister. He studied at Cambridge College, and married **Anne Dudley** in 1628. She was the daughter of Thomas Dudley and the half-sister of **Joseph Dudley** (see no. 57). The Bradstreets immigrated to Boston in 1630. They moved from Boston to Ipswich, and then to North Andover in 1644, which at the time, placed them close to the frontier. The couple had eight children, and left numerous descendants; Supreme Court Justice **Oliver Wendell Holmes** was one of them.

Anne began to write poetry in her middle years. Her brother-in-law published her work without her knowledge in 1650, as *The Tenth Muse, Lately Sprung Up in America*. Her collection of poems—about scientific and moral and religious themes—was the first original poetry written by a colonist. Her more subjective feelings were expressed in a poems dedicated to her family. For example, she addressed these words to her husband: "If ever two were one, then surely we/ If ever man was loved by wife, then thee/ If ever wife was happy in a man/ Compare with me, ye women, if you can."

After Anne's death, Simon continued to serve in the political affairs of the Massachusetts Bay Colony, and was elected governor in 1679. His rise to power came at a time when the Puritan colony was under close supervision by the mother country. In fact, King Charles II was looking for any good reason to annul the colony's charter. A loyal Puritan, Bradstreet wanted to prevent this.

In 1686, King James II, who had succeeded his brother Charles II on the throne, annulled the charter and created the Dominion of New England. The new royal governor, Sir **Edmund Andros** (see no. 47) appointed Bradstreet a councilor, but Bradstreet declined the post. He remained in political hiatus until 1689 when Andros was overthrown in a one-day revolt. Bradstreet was elected head of the provisional government that awaited confirmation of the revolt from England.

The last crisis that Bradstreet confronted was the **Salem Witch Trials**. His own feelings on the matter are unknown, but he consented to the imprisonment of the suspects. Bradstreet finally was able to step down from office late in 1691, when Sir William Phips arrived as the new royal governor.

Bradstreet married a second time, to Ann Downing Gardner. He died in 1697, a visible relic from the hallowed days of the Puritan migration of the 1630s.

Simon Bradstreet

The most renowned of the Puritan missionaries, **John Eliot** was born in Widford, a village near London, in 1604. The third of seven children, he earned his bachelor's degree at Jesus College in 1622. Around 1630, he fell under the spiritual influence of **Thomas Hooker** (see no. 21) and taught at Hooker's school.

In 1631, Eliot sailed on board the *Lyon* for the Massachusetts Bay Colony. He soon took up a post as teacher and pastor of the church of Roxbury, Massachusetts, just outside of Boston. In 1632, he married Hanna Mumford and the couple eventually had six children.

Eliot was interested in the lives and souls of the Native Americans around him, so he learned the **Algonquin** language from an Indian servant in his home. In 1646, Eliot began to preach to the Algonquin in their own language. Hearing of Eliot's work, missionaries in England founded the Society for the Propagation of the Gospel, which was charted by Parliament in 1649. The society provided funds for Eliot and others to further their endeavors.

In 1650, Eliot established in **Natick** the first settlement of Native American converts to Christianity. From the start, the Indian converts looked upon Eliot with love; he had a great charm and ease of manner which endeared him to nearly everyone he met. It is said that children almost always found small gifts waiting for them in Eliot's large coat pockets.

Meanwhile, Eliot worked to translate the Old and New Testaments into the Algonquin language. His efforts bore fruit in 1663, when his translation was published in Cambridge. It was the first Bible to be printed anywhere in the American colonies. Eliot wrote a revised edition that was printed in 1685. He also translated many of the classic Puritan texts into the Algonquin language.

King Philip's War came as a disaster to Eliot's mission. By 1675, he had founded 14 different towns of "praying Indians." The war disrupted most of what he had accomplished. His favorite Indian group—those at Natick—were removed to Deer Island in Boston Harbor for the duration of the war. Many died from sickness there. Even after the war ended, Eliot was unable to re-establish his settlements with the success he previously had.

Eliot died in Roxbury, uttering the final words, "Welcome Joy." In his will, he left 75 acres of land for the teaching of Indians and African-Americans in Roxbury. Virtually all who had known Eliot mourned his death. He was one of a small group of unique individuals who were able to move with ease through almost all segments of colonial society and to retain the good will of virtually everyone.

John Eliot

William Berkeley was born in Bruton, Somersetshire, England, to a celebrated family. He graduated from Oxford in 1629 and had some artistic success as a playwright; his play *The Lost Lady* was performed in 1638.

Berkeley went to the Virginia colony as its new royal governor in 1642. He introduced the cultivation of silk, cotton, and rice in an attempt to diversify the colony's economy. In 1644, Berkeley faced an Indian rebellion led by Chief **Opecancanough** (see no. 12). Berkeley led a small troop of cavalry in the campaign that defeated Opechancanough, and he gained considerable popularity in Virginia as a result of his military efforts.

In 1649, King Charles I was beheaded on the order of the English Parliament. Berkeley declared his undying loyalty to the Stuart dynasty, the royal family to which Charles I belonged, and defied the new Commonwealth government. It took a naval force from England to make Berkeley submit in 1652. He lost his position as governor but regained it in 1660, when Charles Stuart ascended the throne as King Charles II.

Berkeley's long second term as governor (1660–1677) was less successful than his first. In 1675, Berkeley lost the approval of many colonists when he refused to authorize a campaign against Native American tribes that menaced the western frontier. **Nathaniel Bacon** (see no. 56) mobilized a militia force and attacked the Indians without Berkeley's permission. The governor denounced Bacon as a rebel. Thus began "**Bacon's Rebellion**," one of the most serious civil disturbances in American colonial history.

To Berkeley's surprise, Bacon won a seat in the new elections for the House of Burgesses. Bacon went to **Jamestown** with 600 followers, demanding a proper commission to fight the Indians. To Berkeley's dismay, he was forced to grant Bacon the commission and

William Berkeley

named him "commander-in-chief" of the militia. However, as soon as Bacon departed for the frontier to do battle with the Indians, Berkeley denounced him once again as a rebel and mobilized forces to oppose him.

When Bacon approached with another army, Berkeley fled Jamestown and sailed across Chesapeake Bay for the Eastern Shore. The rebels took over the government and burned Jamestown to the ground. Berkeley and his small group of loyalists began to carry out raids against the rebels on the mainland when Bacon suddenly died of influenza. After his death, support for the rebellion soon faded.

Berkeley pursued the former rebels with vengeance. Twenty-three rebels were hanged or shot. Recalled to England to defend his actions, Berkeley died soon after his arrival in the mother country, and the issue never came to a hearing.

39. Leonard Calvert
(1606–1647)

Leonard Calvert

Leonard Calvert was born in England in 1606. His father George, an important English lord and the Baron of Baltimore, was a devout Roman Catholic. Seeking to establish a safe haven for Catholics, Lord Baltimore obtained a charter to colonize what eventually became **Maryland**. When George Calvert died just before the charter was issued, his eldest son, Cecil, became the colony's Lord Proprietor. Cecil remained in England and sent his brother Leonard to Maryland, to serve as the first governor of the province.

Leonard Calvert sailed for the New World along with 200 colonists in November, 1633. They landed in March, 1634, and set up the nucleus for the colony at **St. Mary's City**. Even though the charter from King Charles I granted great powers to a Lord Proprietor, Leonard Calvert agreed to the establishment of an assembly of freeholders. That assembly

met in February, 1635 and soon gained the right to initiate legislation on its own accord. The Lord Proprietor retained veto power over the laws passed by the assembly.

Calvert found that the greatest stumbling block to the colony's growth and progress was a Virginian named **William Claiborne** (see no. 23). Claiborne began a controversy over the ownership of Kent Island in Chesapeake Bay, a dispute that would last for more than 20 years and threaten the security of the colony.

Calvert launched an attack on Kent Island while Claiborne was away in February, 1638. Calvert's troops captured the island, but his troubles with Claiborne had only begun. The Virginian continued to harass the Maryland colony.

In 1643, Calvert went to England to confer with his older brother, the Lord Proprietor. During Calvert's absence, Claiborne made an alliance with **Richard Ingle**, an English sea captain, and launched an invasion of the Catholic colony. St. Mary's fell into Claiborne's hands, and the Protestant minority within Maryland welcomed Claiborne and Ingle as heroes.

Calvert sailed from England to Virginia, where he recruited soldiers to fight for his side. He knew he could not rely on support from England because **Oliver Cromwell** and the Puritan government were hostile to his cause. Using Virginian soldiers as mercenaries, Calvert invaded Maryland, defeated both Claiborne and Ingle, and restored the original government to the colony. Shortly after he had done so, Calvert fell ill. He left the governorship to Thomas Green and made **Margaret Brent**, his sister-in-law, his executor (see no. 34). Calvert died in 1647, leaving behind a fragile colony that would eventually grow into the important city of Baltimore.

40. Isaac Jogues
(1607-1646)

Isaac Jogues was born in the city of Orleans, France in 1607. His father died when Isaac was an infant and he was raised by his mother, who was renowned for her piety. In 1624, Jogues joined the Jesuit order, and was ordained as a priest in 1636. In that same year, he left home for French Canada.

When Jogues arrived at Quebec, he found a tiny colony that was just beginning to take root in the Canadian soil. Jogues was sent by his order to Huronia, the country of the **Huron Indians** on the western side of Georgian Bay. During the long canoe trip there, Jogues learned the Huron language. After arriving in Huronia, he started building a new Jesuit mission, called **Ste. Marie**.

In 1641, Jogues went north with his fellow Jesuit Raymbault and a group of Huron. During their journey, they saw a strait they named Sault de Ste. Marie. Unknowingly, Jogues was helping to blaze the trail for what would become one of the principal trade routes of the French fur traders.

In 1642, Jogues and two fellow Jesuits were captured by **Iroquois Indians** while they were on their way from Huronia to Quebec. The Jesuits were taken to the central part of modern-day New York State. His two companions were killed, and Jogues was tortured and then held as a slave for a year. Throughout this period of captivity, he tried to convert his Iroquois captors, who were amazed by his persistence. Jogues was finally rescued by Dutch traders from Albany, and taken to New Amsterdam (modern-day New York City). He took a ship from there and reached the coast of France on Christmas Day 1643.

Jogues became an immediate hero in France. His fellow Jesuits acclaimed him as one of their greatest missionaries. The Queen received him, and the Pope made a special dispensation that allowed Jogues to serve Catholic mass.

Isaac Jogues

Jogues returned to Quebec in 1644. He led an embassy to the Iroquois in 1646. After returning safely from this hazardous endeavor, Jogues asked for and received permission to form a permanent Catholic mission in the country of the **Mohawk Indians**. He went to the Mohawk lands, where he was killed by a blow from a tomahawk. Jogues was made a saint in 1930 and is included in the list of "Canadian Martyrs."

41. Mary Dyer
(c. 1610–1660)

One of the **Quaker** martyrs who died for the cause of religious freedom, **Mary Dyer** was born Mary Barrett in England. The circumstances of her upbringing are unknown, though it seems likely she came from a family with money and received a good education.

Mary Barrett married William Dyer, a milliner, at St. Martin's-in-the Field Church in London in 1633. The couple crossed the Atlantic and arrived in Boston in 1635, where they immediately joined the **Puritan** church. Mary Dyer soon showed herself to be a "freethinker." A friend and follower of **Anne Marbury Hutchinson** (see no. 26), Mary was supposedly the only person to rise and accompany Hutchinson out of the church when she was banished in 1638. Subsequently, Mary Dyer and her husband were also banished from the Massachusetts Bay Colony.

The Dyers accompanied Hutchinson to Rhode Island, where he became a colonial officer and they raised five sons. They lived a routine life until 1652, when William and Mary went on a trip to England. He returned within a year, but Mary stayed in England until 1657. During that time she joined the Society of Friends— the Quakers. When she returned to New England, Mary was a true Quaker evangelist, preaching about the "Inner Light."

In 1658, During that same year, the Massachusetts legislature passed, by one vote, an ordinance that banished all Quakers on pain of death. Rather than putting fear into the Quakers, the new law seemed to summon up even stronger resistance.

In 1659, Mary Dyer went to Boston to comfort two Quakers being held in the Boston jail. She was banished along with them. All three of the Quakers soon returned to Boston and were sentenced to die. On October 27, 1659, Dyer was led to the gallows and watched as her two co-believers were hanged. She received a last minute reprieve, and was sent away for the third time.

Mary returned to Boston in May, 1660 and began to preach once more. She said she wished to "offer up her life" in protest of a "wicked law against God's people." This time there was no reprieve. Mary Dyer was tried and executed on June 1, 1660. To the very end, she was calm, as if she welcomed whatever trials came to her in the practice of her faith.

Soon after Mary's death, King **Charles II** sent an order to the Massachusetts Bay Colony, requiring that all Quakers be sent to England for trial. No more executions took place. In 1959, the Massachusetts legislature voted that a statue of Mary Dyer be placed on the grounds of the Massachusetts State House.

Mary Dyer

The man who became known as **"Old Silver-Leg"** was born around 1610 at Peperga, in Friesland, in the United Provinces of the Netherlands. He was the son of a pastor of the Dutch Reformed church.

Peter Stuyvesant entered the service of the **Dutch West India Company** at an early age. As a military employee of the company, he was sent to the island of Curacao, 60 miles north of Venezuela. Stuyvesant passed several pleasant and rather routine years there before he was made governor of the island in 1643.

During the **Thirty Years' War** between the Netherlands and Spain, Stuyvesant planned and then led an assault on the Spanish island of St. Martin in 1644. The attack was repelled and Stuyvesant returned to Curacao with a wound in his right leg. The leg was amputated and replaced by a silver-ornamented wooden leg.

In 1646, Stuyvesant was named governor of New Netherland. Arriving at **New Amsterdam** in May 1647, he soon showed himself to be a leader of great energy and vision. He had the streets straightened and a wooden palisade erected to defend the town. A wooden wharf was constructed as well.

However, Stuyvesant could find no solution to the colony's two most pressing problems: its small population, and encroachment by settlers from New England. The Netherlands were extremely prosperous in the mid-seventeenth century and few Dutchmen could be persuaded to emigrate to the New World. At the same time, New England was expanding onto Long Island and threatening the safety of New Netherland.

Stuyvesant also faced internal troubles. The citizens of New Amsterdam forced him to grant independent municipal control to a board of select men. Therefore, the governor could not even give orders within the major town of the colony.

Peter Stuyvesant

In 1655, Stuyvesant undertook a short campaign that conquered the colony of **New Sweden** in modern-day Delaware. His triumph was unmistakable, but it was also short-lived. In 1664, a fleet of English ships led by Colonel **Richard Nicoll**s anchored in the harbor of New Amsterdam. Speaking for his patron, the Duke of York, Nicolls demanded the surrender of the town.

The town council refused to fight. When Stuyvesant ripped a letter from Nicolls to shreds, the councilmen gathered the pieces of paper, and joined them together. To his dismay, Stuyvesant had to surrender the colony without a fight.

Stuyvesant returned to the Netherlands in 1665. He successfully defended his actions before the Dutch West India Company, and was allowed to retire from public service. He returned to his former home in what had then become New York, and lived the rest of his life as a Dutch subject in an English colony.

Paul Maisonneuve, the founder of Montreal, was born at Neuville-sur-Vanne in the province of Champagne in France, and grew up in the manor house belonging to his family. Like many of his ancestors before him, Maisonneuve entered the French military as a young man. Little is known of his duties, but he probably saw action during the Thirty Years' War which raged in Europe between 1618 and 1648.

In 1641, the Company of Notre-Dame de Montreal selected him to head the creation of a new settlement in Canada. Up to this time, the only significant French settlement was at Quebec, which had been founded on the site the Laurentian Iroquois had called Stadacona. Maisonneuve sailed from France and arrived at Quebec in August, 1641.

In the spring of 1642, Maisonneuve and members of his company sailed southwest from Quebec and arrived at the large island where the native settlement of Hochelaga had been in 1535 when **Jacques Cartier** first visited the site (see no. 4). On May 18, 1642, Maissoneueve founded the settlement of Ville-Marie on the narrow strip of land directly under the mountain the French called **Mont Real**.

Toward the end of 1642, the town was threatened by severe flooding from the St. Lawrence River. As the flood waters lapped at the edges of the palisade built around the settlement, Maisonneuve made a solemn vow that if the town was spared, he would walk to the top of Mont Real with a cross upon his back in a simulation of Jesus

Christ's walk up Calvary. The waters did recede and Maisonneuve made his historic walk up the mountain in the spring of 1643. His actions commemorated a distinctly pious attitude that would remain a hallmark of Montreal in the years to come.

Maissoneuve successfully fended off another threat in 1643; this time the danger came from an attack by the **Iroquois**. Maisonneuve returned to France in 1645, to settle the business affairs of his late father, and then he returned to Montreal. Maisonneuve remained governor of the settlement until 1663, when New France became a royal colony under the jurisdiction of King Louis XIV. France declared an official policy of expanding New France for the glory and wealth of the mother country. This policy, called **mercantilism**, was initiated by the French finance minister, Jean-Baptist de Colbert. The era of adventurous explorers and pious settlers had come to an end. Maisonneuve returned to France and settled in Paris, where he lived in relative seclusion for the rest of his life.

Montreal in mid-1700's

44. Rebecca Nurse
(1621–1692)

Rebecca Nurse's house

Rebecca Towne was born in Great Yarmouth, England, the eldest child in her family. She came to the Massachusetts Bay Colony around 1643, married **Francis Nurse**, a tray-maker, and they eventually had eight children.

In 1678, Francis and Rebecca bought a large farm in **Salem Village** (modern-day Danvers, Massachusetts). While Francis prospered in business, the Nurse family became involved in several land disputes; one family they tangled with was the Putnams.

During the winter of 1692, a number of young girls in Salem began to act strangely; they twitched and convulsed, almost as if they were possessed, acting on cue from some hidden spirits. Twelve-year old **Ann Putnam** was one of those who behaved this way. Soon the girls were claiming that certain members of the community were to blame for their behavior. Before long the townspeople began to arrest the people the girls named on charges of witchcraft.

To nearly everyone's surprise, Rebecca Nurse was accused of being a witch. Even though 38 members of the community signed a petition attesting to her moral character, she was arrested on March 24, 1692, at the request of the Putnam family.

A group of women examined her, and announced they had found a mark of the devil upon her. Rebecca Nurse responded "I can say before my Eternal Father, I am innocent, and God will prove my innocency."

When Rebecca Nurse went to trial, the jury initially announced it had found her "not guilty." The judges sternly reminded the jurors that **Goody Hobbes**—a woman who had previously confessed to being a witch—had muttered "She is one of us," in reference to Rebecca Nurse.

The jurors withdrew to consider what the judges had told them. When the jury returned, the foreman asked Rebecca Nurse what Hobbes could have meant by "She is one of us." There was no answer from the defendant. The jury then pronounced a sentence of guilty.

When she later learned what had tipped the balance against her, Rebecca said that she had been full of grief at the moment when the jury posed the question to her. She was also hard of hearing and may not have heard the question.

Governor Sir **William Phips** granted a reprieve to Nurse, but prominent Salem leaders asked him to reconsider. When Phips withdrew his objection, Rebecca Nurse was excommunicated from membership in her church and then publicly hanged.

In 1706, Ann Putnam made a written statement of remorse for her part in the trials, and made special mention of Rebecca Nurse. In 1711, the Massachusetts legislature reversed the conviction against Rebecca Nurse and the next year the Salem congregation reinstated her as a member.

Louis de Buade

Louis de Buade, comte de Frontenac et de Pallau was born at Saint-Germain, France, in 1622. He was the only son of an ancient and noble family and King **Louis XIII** was his godfather. He inherited the title of count of Frontenac, and was known by this traditional name.

Frontenac served in the French army during the **Thirty Years' War**, and by the time he was 26 he had been promoted to brigadier general. He fared less well during peacetime, being frequently involved in civil disputes. In a determined effort to escape his creditors, he served in a Franco-Venetian campaign against the Turks on Crete from 1669 to 1670, but he was dismissed after a quarrel with his superiors.

King Louis XIV named Frontenac governor of **French Canada** in 1672. This was indeed fortunate for him, because the job granted him temporary immunity from his creditors.

Frontenac arrived at Quebec the same year and soon instituted a policy of expansion. He had a fort built near the mouth of Lake Ontario; the fort was later named for him. He also encouraged the travels and explorations of **Robert Cavelier de la Salle** (see no. 53).

While governor, Frontenac tangled with the Sovereign Council and the Jesuits, both of which pushed for his replacement. In 1682, he was recalled by King Louis XIV and returned to France. Back in his native country, Frontenac was again besieged by creditors. His life was miserable until 1689, when the start of King William's War between France and England created the need for a military man in Quebec. He went to Canada as governor once again.

During the winter of 1689-1690, Frontenac sent out three war parties composed of French-Canadians and their **Abenaki Indian** allies. The parties carried out successful raids against villages in New York and New England, but they also provoked retribution. The Puritans of the Massachusetts Bay Colony sent 2,200 men in 33 ships to attack Quebec.

Frontenac, who had been in Montreal, reached Quebec just days before the Puritan fleet. The English sent a messenger ashore to demand the surrender of the town. The messenger was blindfolded and led to the Chateau St. Louis where he was received by Frontenac and his military aides. After hearing that the English demanded a surrender within one hour's time, Frontenac answered: "Tell your general that my only reply will be from the barrels of my muskets and the mouths of my cannons!"

The Puritan siege of Quebec was a failure. The English sailed away and New France rejoiced. Frontenac died at Quebec in 1698, one year after the Treaty of Ryswick brought peace between England and France.

46. Mary Rowlandson
(c. 1635–1682)

"The Lord hath showed me the vanity of these outward things.... That we must rely on God himself and our whole dependence must be upon Him... I have learned to look beyond present and smaller troubles and to be quieted under them, as Moses said, Exod.14:13, 'Stand still and see the salvation of the Lord.'"

The author of one of the greatest "captivity narratives," **Mary White** was born, probably in England, around 1635. Almost nothing is known of her early years; her father was one of the original proprietors of the township of Lancaster, Massachusetts. In 1656, she married **Joseph Rowlandson**. He had been the sole graduate of Harvard College in 1652 and he became the first minister of Lancaster. The couple had four children.

The Rowlandsons lived a relatively uneventful life until February 10, 1676, when the warriors of **Metacomet**—called "King Philip" by the English—burst upon the town. This was one of the many raids made on New England villages during what became known as **King Philip's War** (see no. 50). Eleven townspeople were killed and 21 others were taken captive in the attack. Joseph Rowlandson was away that morning and was not captured, but his wife and their three surviving children were taken prisoner. The Indians led the captives away toward western Massachusetts.

Mary Rowlandson's youngest child died of exposure almost as soon as the journey began. During the 11 weeks and five days of captivity that followed, Rowlandson and her two children marched on a journey that took them to what is now Chesterfield, New Hampshire. During their journey, Rowlandson kept a diary of the 20 "removes"—as she called the daily marches and nightly camps—and an account of the grueling hardships she and her children

endured. Still, by obeying their captors—and making shirts and knitting stockings—Rowlandson managed to obtain the good will of some of the Native Americans, including Metacomet.

On May 2, 1676, Mary Rowlandson and her two children were released for a ransom of twenty pounds sterling. "**Redemption Rock**" near the border of Princeton and Westminster, Massachusetts, remains a historic site to the present day.

In 1677, the Rowlandson family moved to Wethersfield, Connecticut, where Joseph Rowlandson became the town minister. He died in 1678, and the town voted an allowance of 30 pounds sterling per year to his widow, for as long as she remained in the village.

In 1682, *The Soveraignty & Goodness of God, Together with the Faithfulness of His Promises Displayed* was published. It contained Mary's diary, and it became an instant success with the highly literate population of Puritan New England.

Colonists hiding from Indian attack

53

47. Edmund Andros
(1637–1714)

Edmund Andros was born in London, England in 1637, the son of an aristocratic family. Andros joined the English army in 1666, and in 1672, he was named one of the original proprietors of **Carolina**, which was later divided into North and South Carolina. By this time, Andros had become a firm friend and client of James, the Duke of York, who appointed Andros governor of the New York colony in 1674.

During his tenure as governor, Andros showed the firm disposition of a military man. When he could not gain solid support from the colony's English settlers, he was called back to England in 1681. He served as lieutenant colonel of the Princess of Denmark's regiment of cavalry until 1686, when his friend—the former Duke of York, now King James II—named him governor-general of the new **Dominion of New England**. The dominion included Maine, New Hampshire, Massachusetts, Rhode Island, and Connecticut.

Andros arrived in Boston in December, 1686 and immediately put in place a new form of government. He assumed the position of governor and he had a council of advisers, but there was no elected assembly. During the next two years, Andros angered officials in Rhode Island and Connecticut who insisted that their original colonial charters guaranteed them certain rights and freedoms.

The people of Massachusetts were restive as well. The town of Ipswich in Essex County refused to pay taxes to Boston, since there was no elected assembly to levy the taxes. Andros threw the chief protester in jail and managed to collect the king's taxes, but even Andros could see that under the circumstances the people of New England were difficult to control.

Meanwhile, in late 1688, the **Glorious Revolution** in England replaced King James

Edmund Andros

II with King William and Queen Mary. When news of this reached Massachusetts, a crowd in Boston began a riot, and this led to a true revolt on April 18, 1689. Andros tried to escape dressed in women's clothing. He was caught by some citizens of Boston and held prisoner at Castle William in Boston Harbor. It was an embarrassing position for the former governor general.

Andros and his advisers were sent back to England where they were acquitted of any wrongdoing. As a clear indication of their approval of Andros's conduct, William and Mary sent him to Virginia as royal governor in 1692. He served there until 1697, and then returned to England. He died in London, and his reputation remains as one of the ablest colonial governors, but also one of the most despised.

48. Jacques Marquette & Louis Jolliet (1637–1675; 1645–1700)

The team of **Jacques Marquette** and **Louis Jolliet** broke new ground in the French effort to colonize the continent of North America. Jacques Marquette was born in Laon, France. He became a Jesuit priest in 1654 and was sent to Canada. After he showed an aptitude for learning Native American languages, he was sent on a mission to the territory of the **Ottawa Indians**. In 1671, he founded the mission of St. Ignace on the north side of the Straits of Mackinac.

Louis Jolliet was born at Beaupre, Quebec. As a young man he entered the Jesuit seminary, but soon gave up the idea of becoming a priest and devoted himself to becoming an explorer instead.

Jolliet became an expert cartographer. In 1672 he was chosen to lead an expedition to locate the mysterious great river south and west of the **Great Lakes** that the Indian tribes called Mississippi, meaning "Father of Waters." Marquette was chosen as the chaplain of the expedition.

They left St. Igance on May 17, 1673, with five other men in two birch-bark canoes. The group went by way of Green Bay and the Fox River, and then followed the Fox River to the Wisconsin River. On June 17, 1673, Marquette and Jolliet entered the much stronger flow of the Mississippi itself; they were the first Frenchmen to see the great river.

The explorers continued south until they reached the mouth of the **Arkansas River**. There they heard from natives that the Mississippi eventually flowed into the Gulf of Mexico. When they also learned that there were Spaniards on the lower banks of the Mississippi, the French party turned around and went north. They returned by way of the Illinois River, and on this trip Father Marquette established the first parish in Illinois, the *Misson of the Immaculate Conception.*

Marquette's strength was depleted by the journey. When he returned to Illinois and attempted to start another mission in 1674—this one among the Illinois tribe—he fell sick with a lung infection. He returned home to his mission at St. Ignace and died there. Because Marquette's diary was preserved, he became the more famous of the two men. Today there are cities, counties, a river, and even a university named after him.

Jolliet returned east. His canoe overturned just above Montreal on July 21, 1673, and all his maps and charts were lost. Jolliet married Claire Bissot in 1675 and went on to own a successful business. The couple lived on Anticosti Island in the Gulf of the **St. Lawrence River**, which had been granted to him as a reward for his work.

Marquette and Jolliet on the Mississippi

49. Increase Mather
(1638–1723)

Increase Mather was born in Dorchester, Massachusetts. His father was the noted minister, **Richard Mather**. Increase graduated from Harvard College in 1656 and crossed the Atlantic to study at Trinity College in Dublin, Ireland. He received his master's degree there in 1658. Mather was in England in 1660, when the Restoration of Charles II (Stuart) to the throne took place. Because of Mather's **Puritan** roots and his negative feelings toward the new King, he returned quickly to the Massachusetts Bay Colony.

Mather became the "teacher" or minister of Boston's Second Church in 1664, and remained in this post for the rest of his long life. He became a fellow of **Harvard College** in 1675, and in 1685 he became president of the college.

The furor over the Massachusetts Bay charter drew Mather into politics around

Increase Mather

1685. King Charles II revoked the charter in 1684, and his brother King James II created the new Dominion of New England in 1686. Mather went to England in 1688 with Sir **William Phips**—whom he had adopted as his protégé—to protest the actions of both kings.

Mather and Phips asked that the old charter be restored. When they made no headway with King James II, Phips returned to Boston. Mather, however, remained in London. He was overjoyed when the **Glorious Revolution** overthrew James II in favor of his daughter and son-in-law, who became Queen Mary and King William.

Phips returned to London in 1691, and he and Mather persuaded King William to grant a new charter to the Massachusetts Bay Colony. Mather nominated Phips as its first governor, and the two sailed for Boston, arriving early in 1692. To their surprise, the new charter was unpopular in Boston. To make matters worse, Mather found that the colony was embroiled in the Salem Witch Trials, in which his son **Cotton Mather** (see no. 66) was involved.

Increase Mather wrote *Cases of Conscience Concerning Evil Spirits* in 1693; his careful presentation did much to lessen the hysteria created by the witch trials. This was, however, Mather's last significant triumph. For the rest of his life, he found himself and the Puritan cause on the defensive. Phips was recalled to England in 1694, and Mather felt as if his efforts for the new charter had been in vain. He lost the presidency of Harvard College in 1701. Everywhere he looked, Mather saw the advance of the new, more liberal Congregational churches as an insult to the piety of the old Puritan faith.

Mather died in 1723. His long career in the ministry and public affairs was matched by few members of his generation.

50. Metacomet
(1639–1676)

Metacomet was born in the territory of the Wampanoag Indians in 1639, the second son of Chief **Massasoit** (see no. 33). Metacomet grew up in an Indian community that struggled to maintain its ancient traditions while at the same time adjust to its new neighbors—the **Pilgrims** at Plymouth, the Puritans at Boston, and the new Quaker colony in Rhode Island.

Massasoit died in 1660, and his position went to Metacomet's older brother, Wamsutta. The new chief asked for a new name for himself and his brother, as a token of their new authority. The Pilgrims called them Alexander and **Philip**, respectively.

Wamsutta died of sickness while he was detained by Plymouth's leaders in 1662. Metacomet suspected that his brother had been poisoned, and thereafter tried to distance himself from the Pilgrims. However, the Pilgrim settlers encroached further and further on Wampanoag land. Suspecting that Metacomet might try to resist, the Pilgrims summoned him to Plymouth in 1671 and forced him to sign a treaty that bound him and his tribe to the authority of the Plymouth colony.

In June 1675, Metacomet led a large band of Wampanoag warriors in a series of raids against the Pilgrim town of Swansea. The English acted more quickly than he expected, and Metacomet was suddenly forced into leading his men in what became known as "**King Philip's War**."

At first the Wampanoags achieved considerable success. Leaving their homeland in modern-day Rhode Island, Metacomet and his warriors attacked 19 towns throughout western Massachusetts, destroying several of them. From his lookout on Sugarloaf Mountain on the east bank of the Connecticut River, Metacomet could see the English movements and he attacked their towns almost at will.

Metacomet

At the same time, the move westward had dire consequences for Metacomet's cause. The English governor in New York, Sir Edmund Andros, stirred up the Iroquois against Metacomet. They crossed the Berkshire Mountains and attacked the Wampanoags, killing many of Metacomet's men. English Captain **William Turner** also led a devastating attack against the Indians on the Connecticut River, killing many women and children.

As his movement began to crumble, Metacomet returned to the Rhode Island area. There he was shot and killed by an Indian serving with the English leader **Benjamin Church** (see no. 51). Metacomet's head was severed from his body and displayed on a pole at Plymouth as a warning to other Native Americans. His wife and son were taken prisoner, and it had long been believed that they were sold into slavery in the West Indies. However, recent research indicates they were hidden by a sympathetic Puritan minister and survived.

Benjamin Church
(1639–1718)

Historians have long noted that the patriots won many Revolutionary War battles by hiding behind trees, fences, and other defenses. They learned this type of fighting—often called "Indian" or "backwoods" warfare—from observing the Native Americans in battle. And it was one colonist—**Benjamin Church**—who learned the value of these Native American skills and brought them to the attention of his fellow colonists.

Church, who was born in Plymouth, Massachusetts, was the son of a carpenter, and he followed his father into that trade. In 1671, he married Alice Southworth. The couple was building a home at Sogkonates, Rhode Island, when disturbances broke out between the settlers and the local tribes. Church managed to persuade the **Sogkonates Indians** to refrain from joining Indian leader **Metacomet** (also known as King Philip) in his war against the settlers. Church then joined the militia raised to fight the war.

Church was wounded twice in the **Great Swamp Fight**, which took place on December 19, 1675. After the battle, he persuaded many Native Americans to join his militia group by offering them the harsh choice of enlistment or slavery. By early 1676, Church had become one of the main leaders of the Massachusetts militia. He advocated fighting the enemy by using Indian methods.

As **King Philip's War** came to a close, the success of Church's methods became obvious. He took King Philip's wife and son prisoner, and on August 12, 1676, Church's force ambushed and killed King Philip himself near Bristol, Rhode Island. After this successful action, Church was renowned as the foremost English-American expert on warfare in North America.

Church returned to a peaceful and uneventful life as a carpenter and farmer. It was not until the start of the French and Indian wars that he emerged again as an important figure. Serving first as a major, and then as a colonel of militia, Church led a total of five expeditions against the French and their Indian allies in Acadia (modern-day Nova Scotia and New Brunswick). He enjoyed some noted successes, but he retired in bitter disappointment in 1704, when he felt his compensation was inadequate to meet the expenses he had poured into his campaigns. Church died near Little Compton after a fall from his horse in 1718.

Church was the first colonist to adopt "Indian-style" warfare. His successes, led many other colonial Americans to adopt the same warfare tactics. The greatest influence of his methods could be seen on April 19, 1775, when thousands of American "Minute Men" harassed the British troops as they retreated from Concord to Boston.

Benjamin Church

Jacob Leisler was born in Frankfurt, Germany, the eldest son of a Calvinist clergyman. At 20, he enlisted as a soldier in the service of the Dutch West India Company. Leisler was sent to New Amsterdam, where he married the well-to-do widow of a ship's carpenter in 1663.

His fortune assured, Leisler led a fairly uneventful life for the next 25 years. He became a merchant and the captain of one of the New York City militias, but he did not attract a great deal of attention. It was the aftereffects of the **Glorious Revolution** in England that thrust Leisler into the spotlight.

William and Mary displaced King James II in 1688 and became joint sovereigns of England. This situation caused unrest within the colonies, and New York's Lieutenant Governor **Francis Nicholson** appointed Leisler to lead the militia in suppressing the trouble in his colony. On May 31, 1689, the New York militia companies banded together and seized the city's fort. Over the next few days, Leisler switched allegiance from Nicholson's government and took over the New York fort on behalf of the new Protestant monarchs. A committee was elected, and Leisler was confirmed first as commander of the fort, and then as commander-in-chief of the colony since Nicholson had fled to England.

Then, in December 1689, long-awaited instructions arrived from William and Mary. However, while the instructions specified that an unknown administrator named Henry Sloughter would be appointed royal governor, they were ambiguous as to who would rule the colony for the time being. Leisler received the instructions, seized upon this opportunity to declare himself lieutenant governor, and took control of the colony.

In February 1690, a French and Indian war party attacked and destroyed Schenectady, New York. Feeling the need for assistance, the citizens of **Albany** asked Leisler for help. He called for a meeting of the colonial governors of Massachusetts Bay, Plymouth, and Connecticut; the meeting was held in New York City in April. Energetic and decisive, Leisler set in motion an ambitious two-pronged campaign to seize French Canada. Although the plan failed, Leisler had begun an important pattern of intercolonial cooperation.

Meanwhile, in January 1691, **Richard Ingoldesby** arrived in New York as the advance guard for the new governor, Henry Sloughter. Leisler refused to surrender his place to Ingoldesby and in March, Leisler hesitated to yield to Sloughter himself. Sloughter captured the fort, and Leisler, his son-in-law Jacob Milborne, and eight others were arrested for treason. They were tried, found guilty, and sentenced to death. Leisler and Milborne were executed on May 17, 1691.

At King **William III's** insistence, Parliament reversed the judgments in 1695, and the properties that had been confiscated were returned to the Leisler family.

King William III

53. Robert La Salle
(1643–1687)

Robert Cavelier, Sieur de La Salle was the second son of a wealthy merchant family of Rouen, France. He studied at a Jesuit college and entered the seminary, but he left abruptly after his father died.

La Salle crossed the Atlantic to the town of **Quebec** in 1666. He received a grant of land on the western side of the island of Montreal, and worked for a time as a gentleman farmer.

In 1669, wanderlust led La Salle west with a group of priests. He met **Louis Jolliet** (see no. 48) and searched in vain for the Ohio River. This first adventure apparently whetted his appetite for more travel, but historians do not know what experiences he had between 1669 and 1673.

In 1673, La Salle became acquainted with the new governor of Canada, **Louis de Buade,** comte de Frontenac (see no. 45). Frontenac sent the younger man to France to obtain a monopoly on the fur trade. On his return to Quebec, La Salle received command of **Fort Frontenac**, at the mouth of Lake Ontario. Following three years at the post, he went again to France, where he was awarded a title of nobility.

La Salle returned to Canada in 1678. In 1682, La Salle took a party of men and began a journey down the **Mississippi River**. The

Assassination of La Salle

Frenchmen reached the mouth of the river, where, on April 9, 1682, La Salle claimed all the lands on either side of the river for King **Louis XIV** and France. It was a grand moment, perhaps the pinnacle of French explorations in North America.

After La Salle returned to Quebec, he went directly from there to France, where he boasted of his successes. La Salle was hailed at the French court at Versailles. He persuaded the king to sponsor an expedition to reach the mouth of the Mississippi River, via the Caribbean and the Gulf of Mexico.

In 1684, La Salle sailed from France with four ships and around 200 colonists. He quarreled with the ship captains and the navigators, and he failed to locate the mouth of the Mississippi. They sailed past its entrances, which were obscured by logs and dirt that looked like rocks from a distance.

Believing they had found the Mississippi delta, La Salle finally landed on the coast of what is now Texas. Two of the ships were wrecked; the other one returned to France. Finally realizing that the river must lie to the east, La Salle began an overland march. However, in 1687 his men mutinied, and killed him on the Brazos River. It was a tragic end for the great explorer.

William Penn was born in London, England, the son of Admiral Sir William Penn. Young William was educated at Christ Church College in Oxford, but was expelled in 1661 for religious "nonconformity." By 1666, Penn had completely drawn away from the Anglican faith and become a member of the Society of Friends, also known as the **Quakers**.

Quakers believed in an "Inner Light" that dwelled in all people. They had no ministers or priests, and they believed strongly in the right of the individual to worship as he pleased. This made their faith seem strange to Protestants and Catholics, and both groups persecuted the Quakers.

Both Penn's father and King Charles II wanted to break his belief, and in 1669 Penn was imprisoned in the Tower of London. There he wrote *No Cross, No Crown*, which stands forth as his most remarkable literary work. Over the next several years he was imprisoned four times for writing his thoughts, attending Quaker meetings and preaching the Quaker beliefs.

In 1681, Penn found a great opportunity to be of service to his faith. Wishing to discharge a debt of money he owed to the late admiral, King Charles II made a grant of land in the New World to Penn. The King's only stipulation was that it be named **Pennsylvania**, in honor of Admiral Penn.

Penn crossed the Atlantic in 1682, and began to lay out the town of Philadelphia. He drew up a Frame of Government that was more liberal than most of the colonial charters. He also established a pattern for fair dealing with the Native Americans that no other colony equaled.

When he returned to England, Penn wrote advertisements for his colony, and distributed them among the farmers of the Palatinate (in modern-day Germany). Many of them responded to the call, and soon the colony became populated by an interesting mix of English Quakers and German Calvinist farmers.

Meanwhile, Penn worked hard to defend his colony's charter. When the Glorious Revolution of 1688 replaced King James II with William and Mary, Penn briefly lost his charter rights. He regained them, though not without a struggle.

Penn returned to Pennsylvania in 1699. He remained in the colony for a year and a half, and then had to return to England, both to defend the charter and to see to his own financial situation. He left his personal secretary, **James Logan** (see no. 69), as his representative in the colony.

In 1712, Penn's health began to fail, and he spent his last years in genteel poverty. He remained serene, convinced that he had played a major part in assuring the right of religious freedom in the colony he had founded.

William Penn

The person who did the most to open the southern part of North America to English settlement was somewhat of a mysterious person. Historians are not certain where **Henry Woodward** was born; the best likelihood is the island of Barbados. His background before he came to the colonies is also obscure, although he appears to have had training as a surgeon and possessed a distinct talent for learning new languages.

Woodward first appeared in North America in 1664, when he accompanied Robert Sandford to the coast of Carolina. Sandford represented the interests of the lord proprietors who intended to colonize the region. Woodward remained after Sandford left, intending to learn the local Native American language. However, he was captured by a Spanish raiding party and taken as a prisoner to **St. Augustine**, Florida.

Woodward flourished in his new environment. He learned Spanish, converted to the Catholic faith, and became the official surgeon at St. Augustine. In 1668, Woodward escaped captivity when the English buccaneer Robert Searles made an attack against St. Augustine.

Woodward spent a year with Searles, and then was shipwrecked on the island of Nevis in the Caribbean. Surviving that mishap, Woodward went to Barbados where he found passage with the fleet that was leaving for the Carolina coast. Woodward found it easy to demonstrate his usefulness to the colonists, and he became their interpreter.

In 1670, Woodward led the first English party to move inland. He located the native village of Cofitachique, a place no other European had seen since the march of **Hernando de Soto** (see no. 5).

Woodward's greatest contribution to the Carolina colony occurred in 1674. He reached the warlike **Westo** tribe on the Savannah River and signed an alliance with them. In the agreement, Woodward and other merchants provided guns and ammunition to the Westo, who then attacked and destroyed Spanish missions along the coast of what is now Georgia.

Woodward went to England in 1682. He obtained a commission to explore even further, and in 1685 he led a dozen Charles Town merchants to the towns of the **Lower Creek Indians** on the middle Chattahoochee River. Woodward returned to Charles Town followed by 150 Native Americans bringing pelts to trade.

Remarkably versatile and diplomatic, he managed to penetrate at least four worlds: the Spanish and English colonists, the buccaneers of the West Indies, the aristocratic lord proprietors, and the Indians of the Southeast. He almost single-handedly created the trade routes that were Carolina's only source of revenue in the early years of the colony.

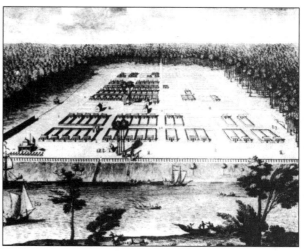

Savannah

Bacon asking Berkeley for aid

Nathaniel Bacon was born at Friston Hall, in Suffolk, England. His father was a prominent English gentleman, and the family was closely related to Lord Francis Bacon, one of the leaders of the growing scientific community in England.

After graduating from Cambridge, Nathaniel married Elizabeth Duke, the daughter of Sir Edward Duke, and the couple emigrated to the **Virginia** colony in 1674. Bacon soon obtained a seat on the Governor's Council. There he found himself in the company of the venerable governor, Sir **William Berkeley** (see no. 38). Relations between the two men were cordial at first, but a crisis along the frontier brought them to conflict.

Bacon had established a plantation at Curl's Neck on the James River. In 1675, he and other frontier planters suffered a series of attacks by the **Pamunkey Indians**, upon whose lands the settlers had intruded. Bacon and his fellow planters asked Berkeley for per-

mission to attack the Pamunkeys. Berkeley refused, suggesting instead that a series of forts would be built to defend the frontier. Bacon and his friends believed that Berkeley made this decision because he valued his trade in beaver skins with the Native Americans

In the spring of 1676, Bacon attacked the Indians without Berkeley's permission and was immediately branded a rebel. Bacon gathered 600 men from the frontier and marched to **Jamestown**. He demanded that Berkeley give him a military commission, and grant new political rights to the planters in the colony. Berkeley was forced to submit. He produced the commission, and the House of Burgesses enacted a series of bills called the "June Laws," which granted most of what Bacon had demanded.

Bacon then left Jamestown in order to again fight the Indians. As soon as he was gone, Berkeley went back on his word. Bacon then returned to the coast and laid Jamestown under siege. Berkeley and his supporters fled the town and reached safety on the eastern shore of the Chesapeake Bay. The colony was in Bacon's hands, and he had his men swear an oath of allegiance to his new government.

However, Native Americans continued to attack along the frontier, and it was soon learned that England would send soldiers to quell the rebellion. In the midst of this, Bacon suddenly took ill and died, probably of dysentery, in late October. Before long, his rebel force had crumbled and Berkeley regained control of the colony.

In the aftermath of the turmoil, the wealthy ruling elite of the colony increased their policy of westward expansion to gain the support of the western planters and prevent another rebellion.

57. Joseph Dudley
(1647–1720)

A colonial governor despised in his home province for his loyalty to England, **Joseph Dudley** nevertheless ably served the interests of the English empire as a whole. Dudley was born in Roxbury, Massachusetts, the seventh child of Governor **Thomas Dudley**. He had two siblings and five half-siblings, one of whom was the poetess **Anne Dudley Bradstreet** (see no. 36).

Dudley graduated from Harvard College in 1665. He served in the Massachusetts legislature from 1677-1682, when he was chosen to go to England. The Massachusetts Bay Colony needed an advocate in the mother country, where King Charles II seemed determined to revoke the colony's charter. Dudley failed in his mission. King Charles revoked the charter in 1684, and a new Dominion of New England was created in 1686, with **Sir Edmund Andros** (see no. 47) as governor.

Once the new charter was in place, Dudley returned to Massachusetts and served on Andros's council. This infuriated many Bostonians, especially when Dudley agreed to the new taxes that Andros laid upon the colony's taxpayers.

In April, 1689, Andros was overthrown by a popular rebellion. Dudley was confined for several months and then sent to England to stand trial on 119 charges. He was acquitted of all of them. To show Dudley that the crown had faith in him, King William named him chief of the New York council. Dudley spent one year in New York, then returned to England, where he served as deputy-governor of the Isle of Wight. In 1692, he returned to Massachusetts, and in 1702 was named the colony's governor.

Dudley found that the Massachusetts legislature was determined to thwart him in every possible way. The Bostonians had long memories, and many of them thought of Dudley as a traitor for having served under Andros.

Joseph Dudley

Whether they were right or wrong, Dudley made few friends during his time as governor. He was always inclined to view the interests of all the English overseas possessions, rather than the particular interests of the Massachusetts province.

In 1709 and 1711, Dudley supported English-American invasions of French Canada. The expansionist party in Massachusetts welcomed his actions, while the conservatives damned his actions as expensive and unnecessary.

Weary from wrangling with his political opponents, Dudley stepped down as governor in 1715. He remained in Boston, and regained some of the popularity as a private citizen that he had lost during his public life.

Popé—a San Juan **Pueblo Indian** medicine man—was the leader of the most successful Native American rebellion of the colonial period. Popé's Pueblo name was "Popyn" which meant "ripe plantings."

Popé was born in the Tewa village of Oke Owinge in modern-day **New Mexico**. In his early years—the middle of the 17th century—Spanish missionaries tried to dissuade the Pueblo Indians from celebrating their religious rites and festivals. This caused great resentment among the Pueblos, a resentment which was aggravated by droughts that ruined their crops.

During this period, the harsh Spanish colonial rulers also provoked bitter feelings among the Native Americans. Popé preached among his people, condemning the loss of territory and cultural customs that had come as a result of Spanish rule. He believed that the Pueblo Gods disapproved of the Spanish and would eventually destroy them. Popé was arrested several times for preaching these beliefs. In 1675, he was flogged in the Santa Fe main square and imprisoned with 47 other medicine men. Eventually, because of many public appeals, the Spanish governor was persuaded to release Popé and his colleagues.

Following his release from prison, Popé went into hiding and organized an armed revolt. The Spanish learned of the plot, so the insurrection began two days earlier than scheduled, on August 10, 1680. The rebels killed 500 Spaniards—priests, settlers, and soldiers were killed indiscriminately. Within a few days, Santa Fe was all that was left of the once-sprawling Spanish colony. Governor Antonio de Otermin decided that discretion was the better part of valor. He led the Spanish survivors south in a retreat across hundreds of miles to what is modern-day **Ciudad Juárez**, Mexico. New Mexico was free and in the hands of Native Americans.

We know very little about the type of government Popé then established. Some stories recount that he became a tyrant among his own people, while others assert that once he had freed his people, Popé went back to being a medicine man.

In 1692, a Spanish expedition forced its way north and reestablished the colony of **Nuevo Mexico**. However, Popé's Revolt had some long-term effects. Although the Spanish reclaimed the region, they never again tried to impose their religion or culture with the brutal force they had used before the Native American insurrection.

Diego de Vargas' troops reconquered New Mexico.

65

William Phips
(1651-1695)

William Phips was born in Wiscasset, Maine, which at that time, was part of the Massachusetts Bay Colony. Around 1672, he found his way to Boston, became a sailor and fisherman, and married Mary Hull, a well-to-do widow.

While living in Boston, Phips learned of a Spanish treasure ship that had sunk off the coast of the island of **Hispaniola** (modern-day Dominican Republic) in 1641. Phips sailed to England and asked King Charles II for a commission and a royal ship to locate the wreck and salvage its treasure.

To nearly everyone's surprise, the king agreed. Phips sailed to Boston in 1684, and then on to the Caribbean, where he searched in vain for the wreckage. He returned to England in 1686 without finding any treasure.

King Charles II had died in 1685, and his successor, King James II, was not interested in Phips's plans. But a group of investors, including the Duke of Albemarle, financed a second voyage.

William Phips

This time Phips hit the jackpot. In January, 1687, he found the wreck of the *Nuestra Senora de la Concepcion*, and by June of that year he was back in London with more than 200,000 pounds sterling of recovered Spanish treasure. It was an incredible fortune, and Phips had salvaged it without the loss of a single man.

King James II knighted Phips; he was the first native-born American to be so honored. Phips returned to Boston and purchased a fine mansion in the most fashionable section of town.

In 1690, war broke out between England and the French and their Indian allies. That spring Phips led a Massachusetts expedition that captured the French post at **Port Royal** (modern-day Annapolis, Nova Scotia). In the late summer, Phips sailed from Boston with 33 ships and 2,200 men, determined to capture Quebec.

Phips arrived at Quebec in early October, just as bad weather was setting in. He made an attempt at a siege, but was thwarted by the French governor **Frontenac** (see no. 45). Phips returned to Boston in November, having lost five ships and around 500 men, mostly to storms at sea.

In 1691, Phips was named the first royal governor of the Province of Massachusetts Bay. He took office in 1692, and was immediately confronted by the Salem witch scare of that year. He created a special court and commissioners to try the witches, but then ended the proceedings after 19 people had been executed.

During his three years as governor (1692–1695), Phips drew the wrath of several groups in Boston. He was recalled to London to defend himself against charges of misgovernance, but died before the matter could be settled.

60. Samuel Sewall
(1652–1730)

An entry in the diary of **Samuel Sewall** for August 19, 1692, reads: "This day George Burrough, John Willard, John Procter, Martha Carrier and George Jacobs were executed at Salem, a very great number of Spectators being present.... All of them said they were innocent, Carrier and all."

Sewall's words show his concern with the **Salem Witch Trials**. He was one of the seven judges who participated in the witchcraft trials. Much of what we know about Boston during the late 17th and early 18th centuries comes from Sewall's diary, which was first published in 1878.

Sewall was born in Bishopstoke, England. His family came to Boston in 1661, and Sewall graduated from Harvard College in 1671. He was ordained as a minister, but soon showed that he had greater interest in public life than in the ministry. Between 1684 and 1686, Sewall sat on the Massachusetts Bay Colony's governor's council. These were

Samuel Sewall

trying times for the Massachusetts Puritans; their charter had been revoked by King Charles II, and they had to submit to the new Dominion of New England government, run by Sir **Edmund Andros**.

When the new charter was approved in 1691, Sewall was again named a member of the governor's council. In June 1692, Governor William Phips named Sewall as one of the special commissioners to investigate the matter of witches in Salem. Sewall played a prominent role in the proceedings, which led to the execution of 19 people.

Later, Sewall found himself overcome with remorse for the deaths. On January 14, 1697, he stood silently in Boston's **Old South Church** while Minister Samuel Willard read aloud Sewall's confession of error and guilt:

"Samuel Sewall, sensible of the reiterated stroke of God upon himself and family; and being sensible, that as to the Guilt contracted upon the opening of the late Comission of Oyer and Terminer at Salem... Desires to take the Blame and shame of it, Asking pardon of men, And especially desiring prayers that God...would pardon that sin and all other his sins." Sewall was the only one of the judges ever to admit wrongdoing.

In 1700, Sewall published *The Selling of Joseph*, a three-page letter that stands as one of the earliest published condemnations of the slave trade. In 1718 he became chief justice of the Massachusetts Supreme Court.

Sewall's diary was discovered in the 19th century and published by the Massachusetts Historical Society. In the diary, Sewall comes across as a man caught between the period of Puritan Boston, with its emphasis on morality, and the new Yankee Boston, which emphasized commercial success. Sewall's words are a vivid portrait of life in colonial Massachusetts.

One of the most remarkable of the royal governors, **Francis Nicholson** faced a variety of challenges during his career. Nicholson was born near Richmond, in Yorkshire, England. He joined the English army at the age of 24, and served for several years in Tangier, Africa. In 1686, he went to America for the first time, as commander of a company of foot soldiers sent to serve under Sir **Edmund Andros**.

Andros named Nicholson as lieutenant governor of the Dominion of New England in 1688. When a revolt broke out in Boston in 1689, Nicholson was in New York City. He yielded control of the town and sailed to England. In order to show that the crown was not displeased with his actions, King William then named Nicholson lieutenant governor of Virginia.

Nicholson spent two years in Virginia, from 1690 to 1692. He helped the Reverend **James Blair** found the College of William and Mary, which became the most prestigious educational institution in the southern colonies.

In 1692, Nicholson was replaced as lieutenant governor by his former mentor, Sir Edmund Andros. After serving as governor of Maryland for four years, Nicholson returned to Virginia in 1698, this time as the full governor.

Nicholson's second administration in Virginia was less successful than his first. He had developed a formidable temper, and he became estranged from some of his former political allies, Reverend Blair among them. He left Virginia in 1705, and retired to England.

Nicholson was called back to service for his country in 1709 when he returned to America to play a role in the planned invasion of French Canada. The campaign was called off for that year, but in 1710 Nicholson led a combined force of British soldiers and American militiamen in the capture of Port Royal (modern-day Annapolis, Nova Scotia). Nicholson served briefly as governor of Nova Scotia in 1712 and then went to England when King **George I** took the throne. In 1720 Nicholson was given one last appointment, as governor of **South Carolina**. There he earned the hostility of the Charles Town merchants. Nicholson and was finally replaced in 1725. He retired to England, where he died three years later.

Francis Nicholson held more posts than any other colonial governor, and while he was not well-loved, he was generally respected for his integrity and sense of duty.

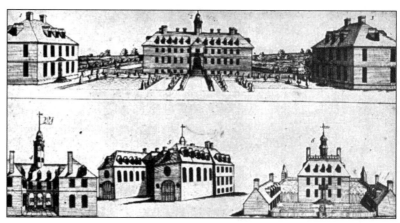

College of William and Mary

Hannah Emerson was born in Haverhill, Massachusetts. She was the daughter of a shoemaker who had emigrated from England, and the oldest of 15 children.

In 1677, Hannah married **Thomas Duston**, a bricklayer and farmer. The couple had 12 children, the last of whom was born in March 1697; three of the children died in early childhood.

On March 15, 1697 a group of Native Americans attacked Haverhill. Thomas Duston spotted the warriors, ran to his house and managed to shepherd his seven oldest children to safety. He had to leave behind his wife Hannah, their one-week old infant, and Mary Neff, a local woman who was working as a nurse for the family.

The attackers seized the two women and baby and took them prisoner. They then began the long trek north toward French Canada where Indians usually held their captives for ransom. On the first day, Hannah was forced to watch while an Indian warrior killed her baby. The Indians then threatened the two women with enslavement.

About 100 miles north of Haverhill, the raiding party stopped at a small island just north of what is now **Concord**, New Hampshire. During a brief pause, Duston and Neff met another captive, Samuel Lennardson, a boy who had been taken from Worcester some time earlier. On the island, there were two native men, three native women, and seven children, as well as the three captives.

At this time, Hannah Duston devised a bold plan. Lennardson had learned from his Indian captor the way to kill and scalp a foe. Hannah decided to put that knowledge to good use.

In the early morning hours of March 30, 1697, Duston and Lennardson used hatchets

Hannah defending herself

to kill their foes in their sleep. Duston killed nine and Lennardson killed one. One woman and one child escaped from the carnage. Duston, Lennardson, and Neff scalped their fallen foes; otherwise, no one would believe their story. Taking a canoe, the three colonists escaped from the island and reached Haverhill safely a few days later.

The entire **Massachusetts Bay** Colony hailed the news. Duston was awarded 25 pounds sterling by the Massachusetts legislature for the scalps; her two companions split another 25. Duston returned to her everyday life in Haverhill and gave birth to a 13th child in 1698.

Two monuments were later built to honor Hannah Duston. One was erected on **Penacook** (or Duston) Island in 1874; the second was erected in **Haverhill**. Both statues show Duston standing with a hatchet in her hand to commemorate the boldness and strength of this captive who fought back.

The Iroquois called him Quidor, meaning "the Indians' friend." To his fellow colonists, he was **Peter Schuyler**—son of a Dutch magistrate from Amsterdam—who rose to become one of the most popular colonial leaders of his day.

Peter Schuyler was born at Albany, in the colony of New Netherland. He was seven years old when the colony changed from Dutch to English hands. He joined the colonial militia at the age of 27, and soon rose to the rank of colonel. In 1686, he became the first mayor of **Albany**.

In his capacity as mayor, Schuyler gained another important position—chairman of the board of Indian commissioners. These commissioners were responsible for all negotiations between the colonies and the **Five Nations of the Iroquois Confederacy**—the Native American tribes who were allied with the English settlers. In the more than 30 years he served as commissioner, Schuyler became a close confidant and friend to the Iroquois. He learned their culture and language, led them in combat, and dealt fairly with them.

In 1689, war broke out between the French and their Indian allies and the English colonies. In 1691, Schuyler—in his role as a major in the militia—led a raid into Canada with 260 men, half English and Dutch militia, and half Iroquois warriors. Schuyler's forces inflicted heavy casualties on the French, killing more than 200 of the enemy while suffering only modest losses themselves.

Over the next several years, Schuyler led many military actions against the French forces. When a treaty ended the war in 1697, Schuyler was sent to Canada to arrange a prisoner exchange of French, English and Indian captives.

For the next 25 years, Schuyler remained very close to the Iroquois tribes and was instrumental in keeping them allied to the

Peter Schuyler

English, despite the best efforts of the French to pull them over to their side. In 1710, Schuyler traveled with four **Mohawk** chiefs to London in order to ask **Queen Anne** for England's help in eliminating the French once and for all. The visit was a sensation. Schuyler had a personal meeting with the Queen, and she offered him a knighthood, which he declined. The queen agreed to send support, but part of the fleet ran into trouble on the high seas and the invasion was called off. By 1712, hostilities had ended and things would remain peaceful between for more than 30 years.

Peter Schuyler died in 1724. He spent much of his adult life in the service of the colonies—helping to defend them against the French, and gaining the respect and admiration of the Iroquois tribes with whom he maintained a long and lasting relationship.

64. Pierre Le Moyne d'Iberville
(1661–1706)

A man who became admired far and wide for his exploits, **Pierre Le Moyne d'Iberville** was born in Montreal, the third of 12 sons of a prosperous merchant. Nearly all of the sons went into public service.

Pierre began his military career in 1686. He distinguished himself on an agonizing overland march to **Hudson Bay**, where the French captured English trading posts. This was only the first of five campaigns that he made to the Hudson Bay region.

King William's War broke out between England and France in 1689. During that winter, Iberville went accompanied a French and Indian war party that devastated the settlement of Schenectady, New York. This action brought retaliation from New York and New England, which sent soldiers against New France that summer and fall.

In the fall of 1690, Pierre was on a mission to Hudson Bay, and therefore did not participate in the successful defense of Quebec. His brother Saint Helene did take part, and was one of the few French killed in the fighting.

In 1694, Iberville led the French expedition that captured York Fort on Hudson Bay. In 1696, he led a French and Native American war party that captured and destroyed **Fort William Henry** at Pemaquid, in what is now Maine. Late that year, he rav-

Pierre Le Moyne d'Iberville

aged the English fishing settlements in Newfoundland.

In the summer of 1697, he won his most remarkable victory and secured his reputation as a brilliant naval commander. Aboard the 56-gun ship Pelican, he defeated three English warships on Hudson Bay. One of the English ships sank, another surrendered, and the third fled. The *Pelican* herself sank, but Iberville survived.

King William's War ended in 1697. In the brief interval of peace that followed, Iberville sailed from France and located the mouth of the **Mississippi River** from the Gulf of Mexico. Although **La Salle** had claimed the Mississippi area for King Louis XIV, it was Iberville and his younger brother **Jean Baptiste** (see no. 72) who truly founded the **Louisiana** colony.

Queen Anne's War between England and France began in 1702, and in 1706 Iberville sailed on his last campaign. He arrived in the Caribbean and captured the English island of Nevis. He intended to continue his string of conquests, but he caught yellow fever and suddenly died in July. He was buried at Havana, Cuba.

Pierre Le Moyne Iberville was a pure warrior whose flair and personal style endeared him to many of his countrymen. He has been called the first truly Canadian hero.

Robert Carter

"Here lies Robin, but not Robin Hood/Here lies Robin, that never was good/Here lies Robin that God has forsaken/Here lies Robin the Devil has taken."

Like many powerful colonial leaders, **Robert Carter** was buried under a large tombstone with flattering phrases carved upon it. However, someone with a less favorable view of the man who had been "King" in Virginia chalked the above lines on Carter's headstone.

Carter was born in Lancaster County, Virginia. His father was a Royalist who had fled from England after the Civil War there, and then accumulated a good deal of property in Virginia. When Robert's father and then his older brother died, he was left to carry on the family name in Virginia.

Carter was elected to the **House of Burgesses** in 1691. He served there through most of the decade, and was twice chosen as speaker of the House. In 1699, he was named to the Governor's Council, and later served as its president.

Already a man of wealth and influence, Carter benefited to an extraordinary degree from his next appointment. The Fairfax family—proprietors of the Northern Neck, the peninsula bounded by Chesapeake Bay and the Potomac and Rappahannock Rivers—named him as their agent. Carter flourished in this position. While he did not hold any title of nobility, he began to act as if he was royalty. He built up his estate to an extraordinary degree. At the time of his death he left more than 300,000 acres of land, 1,000 slaves, and 10,000 pounds sterling. It was a remarkable achievement in a land where paper currency and buying on credit was standard for most of the tobacco farmers. Carter was both the biggest merchant and the biggest tobacco planter of his day.

Carter was a friend and benefactor of the **College of William and Mary.** At his own expense, he had Christ Church built in Lancaster County. One-fourth of the building was reserved for the use of him, his family, his tenants, and slaves.

Carter married twice. His first wife, Judith Armistead, died in 1699; his second wife, Elizabeth Landon, died in 1710. His children and grandchildren married into the other first families of Virginia, and two Presidents, one United States Chief Justice, six governors of Virginia, and General **Robert E. Lee** were among his many descendants.

Cotton Mather was born in Boston, Massachusetts, the eldest son of Reverend **Increase Mather** (see no. 49). Cotton entered Harvard College at the age of 12; he was the youngest student ever to enroll. He graduated in 1678 and went through a brief but painful period in which he doubted his true mission in life. His severe stammer seemed to rule out the ministry, but Mather overcame his speech impediment and in 1685 he joined his father as co-pastor of the Second Church of Boston.

Increase Mather went to England in 1688. When the colony's situation deteriorated under the policies of Sir **Edmund Andros**, Cotton became a ringleader of the resistance against Andros. He wrote "The Declaration of the Gentlemen, Merchants, and Inhabitants of Boston," which became the manifesto of the revolt. In 1690, Mather baptized Sir **William Phips**. By bringing Phips into the fold of the faithful Puritans, Mather created an alliance that would influence much of the middle part of Mather's career.

In 1692, Increase Mather returned to Boston with a new charter for the Massachusetts Bay Colony. Phips became the first royal governor, and the victory of the Mathers and their champion seemed complete.

Ugly tales of witchcraft in **Salem** soon reached Boston, and the Salem trials were held in the summer and fall of 1692. Cotton Mather took a moderate stand toward the situation. He announced his belief that fasting and prayer were better remedies than punitive legal actions. However, when 19 "witches" were hanged, Mather wrote pamphlets defending the actions of the judges.

After Phips was recalled to London in 1694, Mather found fewer political supporters in Boston. As his political influence waned, Mather turned once more to religion, but his was the religion of an educated and sophisti-

Cotton Mather

cated man. Deeply interested in science, he wrote *The Christian Philosopher* (1721), a book about science and religious faith. He was also elected to the **Royal Society of London**, an honor shared by only a handful of other colonial Americans. When Boston was struck by **smallpox** in 1721, Mather remembered that his African-American slave Onesimus, had told him about inoculations. Mather then interested a local doctor in the method, and he used it to save the lives of hundreds of people.

Mather endured personal tragedy in his life. He was married three times; two wives died before him, and his third became mentally ill. Only two of his 15 children survived him. Still, Mather remained a faithful Puritan to the end of his life, one who lamented what he saw as the loss of faith by many people of his generation.

67. John Williams
(1664–1729)

John Williams was born in Roxbury, Massachusetts. He graduated from Harvard College in 1683 and taught school for two years before he was asked to go to the frontier town of Deerfield, Massachusetts, and serve as its first pastor.

Williams arriving at Deerfield in 1686, and was formally ordained in 1688. In the interval, he married Eunice Mather, daughter of an important minister of Northampton, Massachusetts, and a cousin of the influential Mather family. John and Eunice had a large family, and they became known as models of faith in the little town.

Tragedy struck Deerfield in the early morning hours of February 29, 1704. A large war party of French Canadians and **Abenaki Indians** attacked the town. The blow came as a great surprise to the villagers. They had believed they were safe that winter, due to the huge snow drifts; they did not anticipate that their enemies would use snowshoes to make their way south from Montreal.

The raiders took 109 prisoners and killed 44 others; 133 people managed to escape. Williams, his wife, and several of their children were seized in their house. The victorious French and Indians then marched their captives north to Canada.

Only a few miles out of Deerfield, Williams's beloved wife Eunice was killed; she had given birth only seven weeks earlier and was not strong enough to make the march. Most of the other captives, including the rest of the Williamses, survived the grueling march to Fort Chambly, just over the border in Canada.

For the next two years, Williams worked hard to keep his family and his flock together. He sternly resisted all efforts by the French to convert him to Catholicism, but he suffered intense grief when his 15-year old son Stephen converted. Stephen Williams later returned to the Puritan faith.

Governor **Joseph Dudley** of Massachusetts made every effort to ransom the captives. His efforts were finally successful in November 1706, when Williams and 59 of the Deerfield captives returned to Boston by ship. Another 29 captives remained in Canada; most of them never returned. One such captive was Williams's youngest daughter, Eunice Williams, who married a Caughnawagna **Mohawk Indian** and chose to stay in Canada.

Williams wrote the story of his ordeal, *The Redeemed Captive Returning to Zion*, while he was recovering in Boston. He then returned to Deerfield and resumed his place as the minister. He married Abigail Bissell in 1707. Williams's book—read by thousands of people during the 18th century—ensured his place in Puritan history.

Indian raid on Deerfield

January 1, 1710

"I rose at 6 o'clock and read a chapter in Hebrew and two chapters in the Greek Testament… In the afternoon we took a walk about the plantation. The weather was very warm. In the evening we drank a bottle of wine and were merry. I said my prayers and had good health, good thoughts, and good humor, thanks be to God Almighty."

Our knowledge of plantation life in colonial **Virginia** would be much poorer if we did not have the diary of **William Byrd**, who wrote in great detail about the events of his life.

Byrd was born in Virginia, the son of a prominent Virginia planter. He left home at the age of six and spent a number of years in England. There he became a lawyer and learned the manners of an English gentleman. Byrd returned to Virginia in 1696, and was soon elected to a seat in the **House of Burgesses**.

Byrd remained in Virginia for only a year. He then returned to England with the title of colonial agent, which meant that he was there to represent the colony's interests in the mother country. Few colonial Americans were better suited to this task than Byrd; he seemed to understand almost instinctively how to maneuver in the complicated world of English politics.

Byrd returned to his home colony around 1704. He married Lucy Parke in 1706, and they had four children. He was named to sit on the Virginia Council of State in 1709. He soon became embroiled in a long and destructive controversy with Governor **Alexander Spotswood.** The new governor wanted to end the long monopoly that planter families had held in regard to owning large tracts of land. Spotswood tried to enforce the policy of "quitrents" which would have prevented the planters from acting as absentee owners.

Spotswood also tried to take away the Council of State's judicial powers.

As a member of one of the great planter families, Byrd strongly opposed Spotswood's policies. He led the resistance to them, and traveled to England in 1715 to express the views of his fellow plantation owners. Byrd and his fellows won their cause mostly through default; Governor Spotswood left Virginia in 1722.

Lucy Byrd died in 1716, William married Maria Taylor while in London, and the couple had four children. Byrd returned to Virginia in 1727 to spend the rest of his life at Westover, his magnificent estate. Byrd laid out the plans for the town of **Richmond**, Virginia, and served as president of the Council from 1743 until his death the following year.

William Byrd

James Logan was a colonist who exhibited a mixture of Quaker piety and down-to-earth business practicality. He was born in Lurgan, County Armagh, Ireland, the son of a Quaker schoolmaster. The family moved to Bristol, England in 1690, where Logan became first a school teacher and then a linen merchant. Toward the end of the century, he attracted the attention of the great Quaker leader **William Penn** (see no. 54), who hired Logan to be his private secretary.

Logan and Penn arrived in Philadelphia in 1699. By the time Penn left to return to England in 1701, he had named Logan as clerk of the colonial council and secretary of the province. Logan soon became Penn's representative during Penn's absence from the colony.

For Logan, representing Penn was no easy task. Many Pennsylvania settlers resented the Penns' privileges, and saw the Pennsylvania assembly as the vehicle with which to combat Penn, and in his absence, Logan. David Lloyd, speaker of the assembly, even threatened to impeach Logan. Faced with this personal grudge, Logan went to England in 1709.

Logan returned to the colony in 1711 and settled in Philadelphia. Three years later he married Sarah Reed, a woman less than half his age. Logan began to use his many colonial

James Logan

positions to make money through the fur trade, and he prospered. Logan found time to pursue other interests; he read Isaac Newton's writings which exposed him to the scientific beliefs of the **European Enlightenment**. Logan then turned to the classic works of Arab astronomy and medicine. Logan accumulated a large library, and he became perhaps the foremost classical scholar in colonial America.

While he was in his 50s, Logan slipped on ice and suffered a bad fall. He never fully recovered, and lived the rest of his life a cripple. Yet despite his injury—and the time he devoted to his business and scholarly pursuits—Logan remained remarkably active in public life. He served as mayor of Philadelphia (1722), justice of Philadelphia County (1726), chief justice of the Pennsylvania supreme court (1731-39) and acting governor of Pennsylvania (1736--38).

Logan finally retired from public life in 1747. He spent his remaining years devoting himself to the study of natural science and reading the classics, to which he contributed his own translations of the Roman politician **Cato**. The plant family *Loganiaceae* was named to honor him.

70. Zabadiel Boylston
(1679–1766)

Zabadiel Boylston, colonial America's most famous doctor, never earned a medical degree. Born at Muddy River (modern-day Brookline), Massachusetts, he studied first with his father and then with Doctor John Cutler in Boston.

Boylston began his medical career around 1700. From the start he was noted for his inventiveness, his willingness to try new methods—and for his eagerness to acquire a great deal of money. However, like all good physicians, he was also concerned with the health and well-being of the members of his community.

Public health, or lack of it, was a serious concern in the colonies. One of the most devastating diseases that periodically swept through the colonies was the dreaded smallpox. Boston endured a severe **smallpox** epidemic in 1702. Boylston was one of those who contracted the disease, but he survived. Nineteen years later, a new generation of Bostonians with no immunity to the disease faced a return of the smallpox.

The disease came to Boston on April 15, 1721, carried by crew members on a ship that arrived from the **Caribbean**. The disease spread rapidly in the small city; soon the well being of the entire community was in peril.

Boylston learned of a new and controversial method of fighting off the disease—a process called **inoculation**—from the community's renowned spiritual leader, **Cotton Mather**. Boylston took up the challenge. On June 26, he inoculated his son Thomas and seven other citizens. Boylston did not inoculate himself since he had already had smallpox in 1702.

Mather and Boylston came under intense criticism from Bostonians who mistrusted this new way of fighting the pox. Both men's houses came under attack, and Mather had to issue several pamphlets in their defense.

Boylston continued to inoculate people despite the town uproar. Over the next several months, he produced his medical records: he inoculated a total of 241 people; only six of them died from the pox, and four of those already had smallpox when they were inoculated. By contrast, of the 5,889 uninoculated people in Boston who contracted the disease, 844 died.

News of the success of inoculation spread quickly, and Boylston was invited to England, where he was elected a fellow of the **Royal Society** in 1726. Before he returned to Massachusetts that same year, Boylston published *An Historical Account of the Small-Pox Inoculated in New England*. Even today, the work is considered a model of objective medical reporting.

Boylston eventually retired and lived quietly on a farm in his remaining years.

Samllpox devasted Boston in the early 1700s.

One of the most colorful—and dangerous—men of the colonial period was **Edward Teach**—better known as the pirate **Blackbeard**. Almost nothing is known for certain about his life until he first surfaced as a pirate in the West Indies in 1716. Some evidence suggests he was born in Bristol, England, a major English port. It is also believed that he sailed in the West Indies as a ship captain and privateer—kind of a black market merchant working for the benefit of the crown—during **Queen Anne's War** between 1702 and 1713. When the war ended, Teach became a pirate acting solely for his own gain.

By 1717, Teach had captured a French ship and converted it into his own private warship which he named *Queen Anne's Revenge*. In the months that followed, he commanded a small flotilla of pirate ships that cruised throughout the West Indies. They sailed along the **Spanish Main**—the routes taken by Spanish ships going to and from their colonies in Central and South America—and then up the coast of North America to Carolina and Virginia.

That spring, Blackbeard— so named for his prominent and lengthy black beard—sent some of his men into what was then **Charles Town**, Carolina, demanding that the inhabitants give them a complete chest of valuable medicines. When Blackbeard had what he wanted, he continued up the coast of

Blackbeard

Carolina, where his ship was wrecked by a storm. Blackbeard escaped in one of his smaller vessels and made his way to modern-day Bath, North Carolina.

He then set up a base on the Pamlico River on the northern coast of North Carolina and proceeded to attack ships offshore. He also forced ships passing up or down the Pamlico to pay him a fee. Supposedly, Blackbeard was paying bribes to the Carolina governor, **Charles Eden**, who allowed the piracy to continue.

The merchants, plantation owners, and shippers were furious at this situation. Finding no satisfaction from Governor Eden, they turned to Virginia, where Lieutenant Governor Alexander Spottswood assigned two British ships to Lieutenant **Robert Maynard**. Maynard sailed to North Carolina, and on November 22, 1718, confronted Blackbeard in the inlet of Ocracoke Island, off Pamlico Sound. A fierce battle ensued, during which Maynard shot and killed Blackbeard. Maynard then ordered the pirate's head severed and tied to the bowsprit of his own ship.

The legend of Blackbeard continued after his death. It was soon rumored that he had deposited large amounts of gold and other treasures on some beach along the coast. Many people have sought this buried treasure over the years—all to no avail.

72. Jean Baptiste Le Moyne de Bienville (1680–1768)

Jean Baptiste Le Moyne, Sieur de Bienville was born in Ville-Marie, the present-day Montreal, the youngest of the 12 sons of Charles Le Moyne, a wealthy merchant. All of the sons eventually served the colony of **New France**, some as soldiers or sailors, others as merchants or adventurers. Both of Jean Baptiste's parents died when he was young, and his older brother Charles acted as his caretaker. However, Jean Baptiste yearned to imitate the successful military exploits of his older brother Pierre; therefore, he joined the French navy in 1692 as a midshipman.

Jean Baptiste served under Pierre's command in some spectacular naval victories over the English off the coast of Maine and then in Newfoundland. In 1698, they turned their attention to exploration and discovery. That year, they sailed from France, and in March, 1699 they became the first Frenchmen to locate the mouth of the **Mississippi River** from the sea. (La Salle had located it by floating down the river in 1682.) Together the brothers founded the colony of **Louisiana**.

When Pierre returned to France, Jean Baptiste remained in Louisiana. In 1701, he served as acting commandant of the colony and then became its commander in 1706. Jean Baptiste built Fort Louis on Mobile Bay, and planned further extensions of the colony. Knowing that the colony needed to establish a more secure central town, Bienville also chose the site that became **New Orleans** in 1718. He laid out the early plans for the town, and remained committed to its growth. Eventually, Pierre and Jean Baptiste were honored by street names and the names of squares in the Crescent City.

In 1717, Bienville was appointed to the newly created position of commandant general. Under his rule, the colony imported black slaves and Bienville promoted the Code Noir (Black Code). Although the law was strict, it was humane for its time, given the standards that existed in the Caribbean.

Jean Baptiste was not as successful in his dealings with the Native Americans. After his defeat by the **Natchez Indians**, the French court recalled him to Paris. In 1726, He was dismissed as commandant general and stripped of all his titles.

Jean Baptiste lived quietly in Paris until 1733, when he returned to Louisiana as governor. While he fought indecisive campaigns against the Natchez and Chickasaw Indians, his knowledge of Indian languages and customs helped build bridges of understanding between the Indian and European cultures and secured the survival of the colony. Jean Baptiste resigned as governor in 1743 and retired to live in Paris.

Jean Baptiste Le Moyne de Bienville

By 1720, the colony of New France had lost much of its valuable fur trade to the English Hudson's Bay Company. One French-Canadian came forward in a valiant effort to reverse that decline: **Pierre Gaultier de Varennes, Sieur de la Verendrye**, later known by his title, Verendrye.

The youngest of eight children, Verendrye was born in Three Rivers, a town midway between Quebec and Montreal. As a young man, Verendrye enlisted in the army, serving in Canada and Newfoundland. In 1708, he went to France, fought in the **War of the Spanish Succession** and was badly wounded at the battle of Malplaquet.

Fur Trapper

Verendrye returned to Canada in 1712. That same year he married Marie-Anne Dandonneau du Sable; the couple had four sons and one daughter. When he saw that his military career had come to a dead end, Verendrye entered the fur trade. Montreal had long been the center for the trade, but the posts of the English Hudson's Bay Company had drawn off the choicest pelts and the largest profits. Verendrye therefore looked to the far west.

In 1727, he was given command of the fur post on Lake Nipigon, north of Lake Superior. There he heard repeated rumors of a "western sea" which he thought would take him to the Pacific Ocean. Verendrye returned to Quebec and persuaded the governor to grant him a commission to find the western sea.

In 1731, Verendrye left Montreal with three of his sons and about 50 French Canadian explorers. During the next 10 years Verendyre and his party established eight new forts in modern-day Manitoba: Forts St. Pierre, Saint Charles, Maurepas, Rouge, Dauphin, Bourbon, Lareine, and La Corne.

In 1738, Verendrye visited the villages of the Mandan Indians on the **Missouri River**. Verendrye experienced frustration and even heartbreak during the course of his explorations. His son Jean Baptiste was killed by Sioux Indians in 1736. Verendrye also ran heavily into debt; the government of New France had granted him a commission to explore, but did not give him funds to do so.

In 1742, two of Verendrye's sons, Louis-Joseph and Francois, went on an expedition that traveled south-by-southwest from Fort Lareine. It is likely that the brothers reached the Big Horn Mountains of modern-day Wyoming in January, 1743, and were therefore the first Europeans to reach the foothills of the **Rocky Mountains**.

Verendrye returned to Montreal in 1743. His health was ruined by his many journeys and he faced bankruptcy. However, as a small consolation, he was made a chevalier of Saint Louis and promoted to captain of the troops of New France just prior to his death.

74. William Shirley
(1694–1771)

Colonial governor and military leader, **William Shirley** was born at Sussex, England, the eldest son of a country gentleman and London textile merchant. He practiced law in London before emigrating to Boston in 1731. By that time he had married Frances Barker, with whom he eventually had nine children.

Over the next ten years, Shirley developed a large law practice, and became associated with wealthy Boston businessmen who were unhappy with the Massachusetts governor, Jonathan Belcher, and wanted to replace him. With the help of his wife, who went to London and acted as his agent, Shirley was appointed royal governor in Belcher's place in 1741.

When **King George's War** broke out in 1744, Shirley was eager for the Massachusetts Bay Colony to fight against France. During the winter he made a daring proposal to the Massachusetts assembly: he wanted to raise a force to attack the French fortress of Louisbourg on **Cape Breton Island**. Shirley's arguments were compelling and persuasive; the assembly passed the measure.

Shirley named **William Pepperrell** to lead the attack on Louisbourg. In early July 1745, when the news reached Boston of the fall of Louisbourg, the town rejoiced wildly. Shirley was credited with having masterminded the British colonies' greatest military triumph.

In 1749, Shirley was sent to France where he worked for three years attending conferences to settle the boundary lines between the French and British colonies in North America. The conferences ultimately failed, and Shirley returned to Boston as royal governor in 1753. War soon broke out again between England and France, and Shirley hoped to play a major role in this conflict—called the **French and Indian War** by the colonials and the Seven Years' War by the Europeans.

Shirley became commander-in-chief of all the British forces in North America after the death of General Edward Braddock in July 1755. However, he feuded with several other important colonial officials, and his planned campaign against the French Fort Niagara failed. When the French won a major victory at Oswego in 1756, Shirley was ordered to return to England and face charges of mismanagement of the war effort.

In England, Shirley was cleared of all the charges, and was then named as governor of the **Bahama Islands**. He served there for eight years, working successfully with the assembly to distribute lands to the poor, encourage new crops, open new ports and roads, and improve the laws. He resigned in 1767—in favor of his son, Thomas—and retired to Roxbury, Massachusetts.

William Shirley

James Oglethorpe
(1696–1785)

The founder of the colony of **Georgia**, **James Oglethorpe** was born in London and graduated from Oxford in 1714. He joined the Austrian army as a foreign soldier, serving with distinction in the Austrian war against the Ottoman Turks.

On his return to England, Oglethorpe was elected to the **House of Commons**. When a friend of his died in debtor's prison, Oglethorpe became aware of the harshness that existed in British prisons. After Oglethorpe made a special report to Parliament in 1729, he was appointed chairman of a committee to investigate prison conditions.

Oglethorpe came to the decision that sending prisoners to work in the colonies was better than letting them rot in jail. In 1732, he and 19 others received a charter from King **George II** to start a colony between the Altamaha and Savannah rivers, just to the south of the colony of South Carolina. The objective of the settlement was to provide a place for debtors, as well as for hard-working poor people who would produce silk and wine for England; in addition, the new colony would stand as a buffer between South Carolina and Spanish Florida.

Oglethorpe arrived in America in 1733 and soon established the town of **Savannah**. He remained there as governor of the colony

James Oglethorpe

for ten years. He had great success in his dealings with the local Native Americans. However, Oglethorpe was well aware that the real threat to the colony's security was the potential danger from Spanish Florida, a danger that loomed larger when Britain and Spain went to war in 1739.

Oglethorpe went south and twice laid siege to the Spanish fort at **St. Augustine**; however, twice he was repelled by the strength of the Spanish defenses. Oglethorpe's greatest success came in 1742, when he routed a major Spanish invading force at the battle of St. Simon's Island. From then on, there was little threat of invasion from the Spanish.

Oglethorpe went to Britain in 1743, and then married an heiress named Elizabeth Wright. Oglethorpe and his fellow trustees of the colony eventually yielded their interest in the settlement to King George II, who made Georgia a royal colony in 1752. Oglethorpe never returned to America.

Oglethorpe was defeated in the elections for Parliament in 1754. He had served for 22 years, holding his seat even for the 10 years that he was in Georgia. He went on to attain notable success in British society, and lived long enough to meet **John Adams**, who came to England in 1785 as the first ambassador from the new nation of the United States.

William Pepperrell
(1696–1759)

William Pepperrell

William Pepperrell was born near the end of the 17th century in Kittery, Maine, which at the time was part of the Massachusetts Bay Colony. Kittery stood at an intersection of trade between New England and Acadia—which later became Nova Scotia—and the Pepperrell family was heavily involved in the shipbuilding, lumber, and fish businesses. William followed his father into business and proved to be an astute businessman. Upon his father's death in 1734, he inherited the bulk of the estate, thus becoming one of the richest men in the colonies.

Pepperrell entered politics as a member of the Massachusetts General Court, rising to the position of chief justice in 1730. In 1727, Pepperrell and his friend **Jonathan Belcher** had been elected to the Governor's Council. When Belcher was named royal governor of Massachusetts in 1731, Pepperrell's influence rose as well. However, that influence seemed to dim when Belcher was replaced as governor in 1741.

The start of **King George's War** brought Pepperrell his chance to attain fame. In the late winter of 1744, the new Governor, William Shirley, persuaded the Council to endorse his idea of sending a fleet and troops from Boston to capture France's Fortress Louisbourg on Cape Breton Island. Shirley saw the wisdom of having the expedition commanded by a merchant who knew the waters off Nova Scotia. Therefore, he offered the command to Pepperrell.

In March 1745, Pepperrell led a fleet of Yankee fishing ships out from Boston Harbor, bound for Cape Breton. They were met by a squadron of the British Royal Navy, led by Commodore **Peter Warren**. Together, the colonial American and British ships sailed to Cape Breton. They landed without opposition, and brought their artillery forward to commence the siege. Fortunately, the French garrison's morale was low, and early on the French abandoned their Grand Battery, the guns of which were soon turned against the fortress.

Commanding the land forces, Pepperrell worked in harmony with Commodore Warren. The two men pushed their troops forward until they were ready to take the town by storm. The French asked to discuss terms of surrender, and on June 17, 1745, the greatest fortress yet built in North America yielded to the joint forces under Pepperrell and Warren.

The news reached both Britain and the American colonies very quickly. Pepperrell was given the English title of baron, the first colonial American to receive that honor. Warren was promoted to admiral.

Pepperrell retired for a time to Kittery. He made one trip to Great Britain in 1752, where King **George II** accorded him great honors. His fame spread throughout the American colonies, and a young George Washington looked on Pepperrell as a model soldier.

Johann Conrad Weiser
(1696–1760)

The most skillful interpreter on the New York and Pennsylvania frontiers, **Johann Conrad Weiser** was born near Wurttemberg, Germany. He came to America in 1710, arriving in New York with his father, siblings, and stepmother as part of a large immigration from Germany.

Resentful of his stepmother, Weiser drifted away from his family as a young man. He spent the winter of 1713 with the Iroquois chief **Quagnant** in the northern part of New York. Weiser then set up his own farm at an Indian village near Schoharie, New York, and found that his ability to speak the Native American language was a distinct advantage on the frontier. Weiser began to interpret for councils between whites and natives. In 1720, he married a **Mohawk** woman; they eventually had 15 children.

Weiser and his family moved to Tulpehocken, Pennsylvania, in 1729. There Weiser met and befriended **James Logan**, one of the colony's top political leaders and administrators. Weiser persuaded Logan that it was in the interest of the Pennsylvania colony to change its long-standing Indian policy. The Quaker colony had long favored the Delaware Indians, with whom **William Penn** (see no. 54) had made his first treaty. With Weiser serving as the go-between, Logan began to make alliances with the **Six Nations of Iroquois**.

Through his friendship with the Oneida chief

A Delaware Indian

Shikellamy, Weiser was able to bring about peace conferences in Philadelphia in 1731 and 1736. By the time the second conference ended, Weiser had created a strong pact between Pennsylvania's Quakers, who were pacifists to the core, and the Six Nations of Iroquois, probably the most warlike of all the Indian tribes.

Weiser continued to play an important role on the frontier. He and the Onondaga Indian Canasatego arranged a treaty in 1742, and in 1743, Weiser managed to prevent a war from breaking out between the Iroquois and the Virginia colony. Weiser also promoted the **Treaty of Lancaster** in 1744, and during King George's War (1744–1748), he and the Quaker government supported the Iroquois who remained neutral and joined neither the French nor the British.

In the late 1740s, Weiser underwent a religious conversion. Born to a Lutheran family, he had joined the Reformed Church at Tulpehocken, Pennsylvania; then in 1735 he was influential in forming a Baptist group in his community. For a time he joined the Solitary Brethren of the Community of Seventh Day Baptists, a radical spiritual community led by Johann Conrad Beissel. After being dissuaded from this group by his family, Weiser returned to a more normal life. He became justice of the peace for Lancaster County, and was probably the only German-American to hold such a post in colonial America.

A colonial pioneer for freedom of the press, **John Peter Zenger** was born in Germany and came to America with his family in 1710. As a young boy, Zenger served an apprenticeship with William Bradford, the official printer of the colony of New York. By the time he was 30, Zenger set up his own printing business, where he specialized in printing Dutch-language works.

William Cosby became the royal governor of New York in 1732. Soon, his policies and his behavior angered many prominent New Yorkers. In 1733, several important colonists sponsored Zenger in his attempt to start a newspaper independent of the colonial government. Zenger's *New-York Weekly Journal* made its first appearance on November 5, 1733. All of the written articles were anonymous, and Zenger took complete responsibility for what was published. For months, the paper strongly criticized Governor Cosby and his group of advisers. This drew the fury of the governor and his council.

On November 17, 1734, Zenger was imprisoned by order of the council. He was charged with seditious libel and held for an enormous bail—three or four times what he made from his paper in an entire year. Zenger remained in prison, and with help still managed to print the newspaper.

When the matter came to trial on August 4, 1735, Zenger's case looked bleak. Then to everyone's surprise, a Philadelphia attorney named **Andrew Hamilton** volunteered to argue Zenger's case. Hamilton was perhaps the most famous trial lawyer in the colonies. From the beginning, Hamilton admitted that Zenger had published the paper; however, Hamilton denied that the charges made in the paper were false. He claimed that for a libel to be proved, it must be both false and malicious. However, the judge—a Cosby appointee—ruled that the only issue in ques-

Zenger's lawyer, Andrew Hamilton

tion was whether Zenger had published the words, not whether the articles were true. Hamilton knew then that his only chance to win his case was through his summation to the jury.

In a stirring speech, Hamilton maintained that the only defense against the wicked and powerful—and the only guarantee of liberty—was to speak and print the truth. Hamilton urged the jury to consider whether it was indeed libel to print statements that were in fact true. When the jury returned, the foreman Thomas Hunt pronounced a loud verdict of "Not Guilty." Zenger was freed.

Zenger went on to become the public printer for New York, and then for New Jersey as well. His case helped establish the right to a free press in North America.

79. Mary Musgrove
(c. 1700–1763)

Creek Indians

Mary Musgrove—"Creek Mary," as the British-Americans called her—was one of the most remarkable people of mixed European and Native American heritage to live on the American frontier.

At her birth in the **Creek Indian** town of Coweta on the Ocmulgee River in what is now Alabama, Mary was given the name **Coosaponakeesa**. Her mother was a Creek Indian from a prominent family, and her father was a British trader. When Coosaponakeesa was seven, her father took her to live among white settlers in **South Carolina**. She was educated there, became a Christian, and at some point began to use the name Mary.

Around 1716, Mary married John Musgrove, Jr. of South Carolina, and by 1733 they were running a trading station among the Creeks. That year, Mary was among the first settlers to greet British colonizer **James Oglethorpe** when he arrived to found the colony of **Georgia**. Mary's linguistic skills, and her knowledge of both the Indian and British-American worlds, persuaded Oglethorpe to make her his chief interpreter and his emissary to the Creek tribes. It was largely due to her influence that the Creeks remained friendly to the British for the rest of the century, thereby allowing the Georgia colony to take root.

John Musgrove died in 1739. Soon after, Mary married Jacob Matthews, one of the soldiers at her trading post. In 1740, she persuaded many of the Creeks to join Oglethorpe in his attack against the Spanish fort at St. Augustine.

Mary and Jacob moved to **Savannah** in 1742, where Jacob died that same year. Oglethorpe left Georgia in 1743. Prior to his departure, he gave Mary 200 pounds sterling and a diamond ring from his own finger, a token of his esteem for the woman who had been so helpful in keeping peace within his colony.

In 1744, Mary married for the third time. Her new husband, Thomas Bosomworth, was a hard-nosed businessman. He and Mary planned to corner the market on cattle in the colony. They obtained a grant from the Creek nation for the islands of St. Catherine's, Ossabaw, and Sapelo, just off the coast of Georgia. Bosomworth stocked **St. Catherine's Island** with cattle he had bought with borrowed money, while Mary presented claims for money to the Georgia colony for her past services.

When Georgia proved reluctant to provide her with money, Mary led a large number of Creek warriors to Savannah and harassed the townspeople there for a month in the summer of 1749. In 1754, Mary and her husband went to Britain to pursue their claims. The matter was finally settled in 1759, when Mary received the title to St. Catherine's Island from the British government.

80. Francisco Menendez
(c. 1700–1772)

Francisco Menendez was born in West Africa. He was enslaved and brought to South Carolina via the infamous "Middle Passage," the route that brought slaves from Africa to the West Indies, and eventually to the colonies. In the 1720s, Menendez escaped from his owners and went inland, where he joined the Yamasee Indians in their war against the white settlers. When the Yamasee were finally defeated, Menendez traveled south with a number of them to take refuge at St. Augustine in Spanish Florida.

St. Augustine was one of the very few havens for escaped slaves in all of North America. Escaped slaves from the north had begun arriving there as early as 1687; in 1733, King Philip V of Spain offered freedom to any escaped slave who would embrace Catholicism and serve a four-year term as a servant in St. Augustine.

Menendez arrived at St. Augustine in 1726, where the Spanish governor named him captain of the slave militia. When it became apparent that Britain and Spain were going to war, Governor Manuel de Montiano established the free settlement of Santa Theresa de la Gracia Real de Mose, just two miles north of St. Augustine. Menendez became known as the "chief" of Mose, and the other free blacks there were his subjects.

In 1740, Menendez and his militia helped Montiano successfully defend St. Augustine when it was attacked by British-American troops. Menendez then served under Montiano in the disastrous attack on the Georgia colony. The Spaniards and their African allies were repulsed at the battle of St. Simon's Island.

However, this defeat hardly discouraged Menendez. He obtained a commission to become a privateer and sailed the Atlantic, where he harassed British shipping. He was eventually captured, tortured, and then sold into slavery in the Bahamas. Rather than accept this fate, Menendez escaped and made his way back to St. Augustine, where he resumed his command of the militia.

One final act of dispossession awaited this hero. In 1763, Spain yielded Florida to Great Britain under the Treaty of Paris. The Spaniards and all their allies, both African and Native American, boarded ships and sailed to Matanzas, Cuba. At the time of the evacuation there were 390 Africans, 87 of them free and 303 slaves.

No one knows what happened to Menendez in Cuba. However, he is remembered as a fearless individual, who overcame the brutality of slavery and triumphed as a brave military hero.

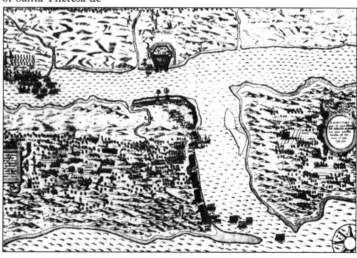

St. Augustine, Florida

81. Jonathan Edwards
(1703–1758)

Jonathan Edwards was born in East Windsor, Connecticut, the only son of Timothy Edwards, a Puritan minister. Jonathan graduated from Yale College in 1720, and earned his master's degree in 1723 at the same school. In 1726, he answered a call to serve as an assistant to his grandfather, the Reverend Solomon Stoddard, of Northampton, Massachusetts. The following year Edwards was ordained as a minister, and married Sarah Pierrepont; eventually they would have 12 children.

Upon the death of his grandfather in 1729, Edwards became the pastor of the Northampton congregation. Although not a loud or fiery speaker, Edwards was a forceful preacher. His parishioners responded to the clarity of his logic and to his convictions. More than most preachers of his day, Edwards was moved by the ideas of the **European Enlightenment**; he saw science and logic as extensions of God's will.

In the early 1740s, a movement known as the "Great Awakening" took place in New England. Churches that had experienced declining membership for years suddenly found new members, and reports of visions of Christ and Satan were widespread. Edwards delivered his greatest sermon, "Sinners in the Hands of an Angry God" at Enfield, Connecticut, in 1741. The sermon was typically Puritanical in that it was based on the belief that a person's salvation or damnation was unknowable to himself. The sermon marked him as a standard bearer for the old **Puritan** cause, but he was in truth much broader in both his mind and spirit.

Throughout the 1740s, in both sermons and publications, Edwards continued to advocate strict standards for admission to the church. Edwards claimed that a man's profession of faith was not sufficient; his life had to show some visible evidence of God's grace for the man to become a true church member. This view brought him into conflict with his Northampton parishioners, and in 1750, they voted to dismiss him.

Edwards and his family moved to Stockbridge, Massachusetts where he served as a missionary to the Native Americans. The family lived in humble poverty for seven years, and Sarah Edwards made do by working as a seamstress.

In 1757, Edwards was asked to serve as the first president of the College of New Jersey, which would later become **Princeton University**. He went to New Jersey, and early in 1758 he took an inoculation for **smallpox**. Edwards hoped his example would encourage others in the community to follow suit. However, the doctor had administered too large a dose in the inoculation and Edwards died. He remains to this day one of America's most influential religious philosophers.

Jonathan Edwards

Christopher Gist was born in Maryland, the son of a surveyor who had helped to lay out the streets of Baltimore. Little is known about Gist's early years; however, it appears from his later work that he received a good education and was especially well trained in map making.

By 1745, Gist had married Sarah Howard, and he moved his family to an area on the Yadkin River in North Carolina, where he became a surveyor, trader, and scout. Five years later, Gist became associated with investors who wanted to open up the **Ohio River** valley to white settlements.

Between 1750 and 1752, Gist traveled through much of the Ohio River valley, working for the Ohio Company of Virginia. He went as far west as the mouth of the Scioto River, helping to lay Virginia's claim to that area.

In 1753, Gist built Gist's Plantation near what is now Mount Braddock, Pennsylvania. It was the first white settlement in the Monongahela River area. That same year, Virginia Governor Robert Dinwiddie sent **George Washington** on a mission to warn the French not to intrude upon British settlement claims in the Ohio area. Washington left Williamsburg, Virginia, on October 30, 1753, and on November 14 he met and hired the experienced Gist as a guide.

Gist and Washington reached the French **Fort LeBoeuf** (near modern-day Waterford, Pennsylvania) in December. Washington delivered his message, and was rebuffed with a warning that the Ohio region belonged to France.

On their return journey, Washington and Gist endured eight days of grueling hardships. Washington nearly drowned once, and was almost killed by hostile natives, Both times Gist saved his life. They arrived at Gist's Plantation on January 2, 1754. Washington then pushed on and reached Williamsburg on January 16, where he delivered the French response to Governor Dinwiddie.

War clouds were brewing. Dinwiddie sent Washington north with a force of Virginia militiamen. Washington's goal was to reach the confluence of the Monongahela and Allegheny rivers, but the French arrived first and started to build **Fort Duquesne** on the site of what later became Pittsburgh.

On May 27, 1754, Gist arrived at Washington's camp and informed him that 50 French soldiers were marching south toward his location. With Gist's information, Washington planned and carried out an attack that resulted in the deaths of 10 Frenchmen, including their leader, Ensign Coulon de Jumonville. This small, backwoods affair set a fire that kindled and grew until France and England declared war against each other in 1756.

Gist went on to serve briefly as deputy superintendent of Indian affairs for the southern colonies. He died of smallpox in 1759.

Gist and Washington on the Monongahela River

Thomas Hutchinson—the great, great, grandson of religious freedom fighter **Anne Marbury Hutchinson** (see no. 26)—was born in Boston to an established merchant family. A precocious child, he entered Harvard at 12, graduated in 1727, and earned his master's degree in 1730. He worked for a time in his father's commercial house before he married Margaret Sanford in 1734. Thomas and Margaret had five children together.

Hutchinson's marriage brought him extensive political connections. He entered the Massachusetts House of Representatives in 1737 and served there for 12 years.

In 1749, Hutchinson was named to the Provincial Council, where he served for the next 15 years. As a leading conservative, he became the enemy of two prominent radicals —later called Patriots — **Samuel Adams** and James Otis. Adams in particular came to see Hutchinson as the embodiment of all that was wrong with the royal government in Massachusetts.

When Hutchinson supported the right of Parliament to levy the **Stamp Tax** in 1765, a Boston mob attacked and burned his home. Despite the attack, Hutchinson continued to uphold the king's government in Massachusetts. He served as lieutenant governor, and then as acting governor between 1769 and 1771, and in 1771 he was made the royal governor of the colony. He was destined to be the last civilian to hold that position.

During his three years as governor, Hutchinson was continually outfoxed by Samuel Adams, who tirelessly incited the people of Boston against the government. Hutchinson made his greatest mistake in December, 1773, when he was faced with a crisis regarding shipments of tea.

Three ships sat in the harbor, full of tea brought from India. Adams and his Boston supporters would not allow the ships to

Thomas Hutchinson

unload their cargo because of the oppressive British tax levied on each pound of tea. Hutchinson would not allow the ships to leave the harbor without having deposited their goods. On the night of December 16, many Bostonians dressed as **Mohawk Indians** took over the three ships, and dumped thousands of pounds of tea into the harbor. The **Boston Tea Party** was a notable success for Samuel Adams, and a dismal defeat for the royal cause in Boston.

In 1774, General **Thomas Gage** replaced Hutchinson as governor. In June, Hutchinson sailed to England; when he arrived he met King George and informed him of the state of near-rebellion in Massachusetts. Hutchinson died in exile in London in 1780. He had loved Massachusetts and America—but he had loved them as a loyal subject of King George III.

Louis-Joseph Montcalm
(1712–1759)

Upon learning that he was dying from his wounds, the great French General Montcalm replied, "So much the better. I shall not live to see the fall of **Quebec**." This hero was the mainstay of French military efforts in Canada during the French and Indian War.

Louis-Joseph de Montcalm was born in Saint Veran, France to a family with a long and distinguished record in the French army. Montcalm entered the service as an ensign in 1724, and fought in the War of the Polish Succession.

The **French and Indian War** began in the colonies in western Pennsylvania in 1754. The conflict spread to Europe, and in 1756 Britain and France began what the Europeans called the Seven Years' War. It was this conflict that brought Montcalm to North America.

Holding the rank of major general, Montcalm arrived at Quebec, the capital of French Canada in 1756. His orders were to

Louis-Joseph Montcalm

hold the colony at all costs against the British. Unfortunately, the colony of New France had a population of only 80,000, while the British colonies to the south had a population of 1.5 million. Nonetheless, at the outset of hostilities Montcalm more than held his own. In 1756, he led a force southwest and captured the British fort on Lake Ontario. The next year, he marched directly south and captured **Fort William Henry** near Lake George. The French victory was marred by the fact that Montcalm's Native American allies attacked and massacred some 200 British troops who were marching away under a British-French truce agreement.

In July 1758, Montcalm and 3,500 French troops successfully defended **Fort Ticonderoga** against a British-American army of 15,000. It was the greatest victory of his career.

However, the tide soon turned against the French. Fort Duquesne in Pennsylvania and Fortress Louisbourg on Cape Breton Island both fell to the British in 1758. By the spring of 1759, the war had reached a crisis point. Later that year, Montcalm prepared to defend the city of Quebec.

With 16,000 men, only 4,000 of whom were seasoned soldiers, Montcalm rebuffed the first attack of British general **James Wolfe**. But on the morning of September 13, Montcalm found that Wolfe had brought 5,000 regular troops onto the **Plains of Abraham**, behind the city's walls.

While the two armies were of roughly equal strength, the discipline and co-ordination of the British troops won the battle. Montcalm was wounded by a musket ball and died the next morning. Despite the defeat, he is remembered as a great military leader who mounted a heroic defense in a valiant effort to save the colony of New France.

Junipero Serra

The founder of nine Spanish missions in California, Father **Junipero Serra** can truly be considered one of the early founders of the American West coast.

Serra was born to a poor family in Petra, Majorca, Spain. An unimposing figure of small stature, the leaders of the **Franciscan** order hesitated before finally accepting him in 1730. Serra soon displayed his intellectual prowess, however. A great orator, he rose to become a professor of moral philosophy, and seemed to have unlimited potential to advance within the order in his native Spain.

However, Serra was possessed by one burning desire—to convert souls to **Christianity**. In 1749, he voluntarily gave up his teaching position and set out for the Spanish colonies in the New World.

Serra arrived at **Mexico City** in 1750. His first assignment as a missionary was among the natives of the Sierra Gorda region, northeast of Queretaro. He labored there for nine years, then returned to Mexico City, where he served as a preacher and confessor.

During the 1760s, under the rule of King **Carlos III**, Spain began to revitalize its overseas empire. When the Jesuits were expelled from Spain and its imperial possessions in 1767, the Franciscans stepped forward to take their place. In 1769, Serra was named "Father President" of the new Franciscan missions to be established in modern-day California.

In 1769, Serra and five of his fellow Franciscans went north with **Gaspar de Portola** as Spain attempted to civilize and Christianize Upper California. On July 16, 1769, Serra and his fellows founded—at **San Diego**— the first of their nine missions.

When Portola returned to Mexico, Serra remained in California. He went on to establish missions at San Carlos Borromeo, San Antonio, San Gabriel, San Luis Obispo, San Francisco de Assisi, **San Juan Capistrano**, Santa Clara, and San Buenaventura. As impressive as this might have appeared, in reality these locations were struggling hamlets, created by a handful of friars who wanted to bring their faith to thousands of Native Americans.

The conversion process moved very slowly. However, by the end of 1783, there were more than 6,800 baptized Native Americans living in the missions. Serra continued his life's work until the very end, even in failing health, traveling frequently to the different missions and working himself harder than he worked anyone else.

In his dedication and solemnity, Junipero Serra was a giant figure in Spain's quest to bring Christianity to the New World.

86. William Johnson
(1714–1774)

William Johnson was born near Dublin, Ireland, and came to America around 1740 to manage the estate of his uncle, Commodore **Peter Warren**. At this estate on the Mohawk River, near Schenectady, New York, Johnson set up a store to handle trade in furs and other items with the natives and settlers. From the outset, Johnson engaged in the two activities that were to mark his entire life: he established good relations with the Native Americans of the region—the **Six Nations of the Iroquois**—and he began to acquire large tracts of Native American land.

Johnson's success in dealing with the Iroquois led the British colonial administration to appoint him superintendent of Indian affairs in upper New York colony in 1744. He also was placed in command of the region's militia forces that played an active role in two wars between the British colonists' and the French and their Indian allies for control of North America—**King George's War** (1744–48) and the French and Indian War (1754–63).

On September 8, 1755, Johnson's troops were near Lake George when they were attacked by a force of French and Native Americans. Johnson's men defeated the French and captured their commander. As a result of this victory, King George II named Johnson a baronet, and he became just the third colonial American to be knighted.

After the war ended in 1763, and the French gave up their North American holdings to the British, Johnson was free to concentrate on relations between the British colonists and the Iroquois. He worked to improve the conditions of life of the Iroquois and to advance peace, negotiating an end to **Pontiac's War**, and the Treaty of Fort Stanwix (1768). The terms of the treaty allowed settlers' to move into Indian territory, and Johnson benefited by increasing his own holdings of native lands.

During these years, Johnson built himself several lavish homes. His most well-known location was **Johnson Hall**, near a settlement that became known as Johnstown, New York. He lived there for his last 12 years like a wealthy landed English aristocrat, with servants and slaves. He also entered into relationships with two Native American women—one of them being Molly Brant, sister of the famous Mohawk chief Joseph Brant. He had 11 children with these women.

Johnson was a self-educated man with a wide variety of interests; he published serious articles on agriculture and Native American languages and customs. Throughout his life, he worked hard to establish good relations with the Native Americans—and at the same time never missed an opportunity to increase his personal fortune.

William Johnson

One of the most famous clergymen and evangelists of the colonial period, **George Whitefield** was born in Gloucester, England. Although many of his ancestors had been clergymen, George's own father was an innkeeper. By his early teens George was already a pious Christian, and when he went to Oxford in 1732, he came under the influence of Charles and John Wesley, the founders of **Methodism**.

The transforming moment of Whitefield's life came during an illness in 1735, when he was filled with a sense of oneness with God and experienced what he called a "new birth." From that point on, he would work to convince others that such an experience was vital to becoming a true Christian. In that sense, he was the founder of "born again" Christianity.

Whitefield soon embarked on the career that would make him famous, a life of constant preaching in any available site, as well as a humanitarian who ministered to the sick and the poor. As an evangelical preacher, he was quite unlike most clergymen of his time; he employed the voice and manner of an actor to excite his audience. Because he did not conform to the teachings of the established **Church of England**, he would spend the rest of his long career under attack from conventional Christians.

In 1738, Whitefield made his first trip to America, landing at **Savannah**, Georgia, which was then a new colony. Here he began his preaching in the colonies, and started the first of his numerous endeavors to found orphanages and schools. The following year, the **Great Awakening** religious movement began, and Whitefield became one of its most prominent leaders. Whitefield's preaching represented the more outward and emotional forms of the Awakening, while its somber and scholarly aspects were presented by Reverend **Jonathan Edwards** (see no. 81).

For the next 30 years, Whitefield traveled back and forth frequently between England and the colonies. Whenever he was in America, he moved up and down the Eastern seaboard giving hundreds of sermons. Whitefield was not an easy person to satisfy or get along with. He became increasingly more rigid in his religious views, and he quarreled not only with other colonial clergymen, but even with John Wesley, the Methodist who had first inspired him. Whitefield was also a man of his time in that while he advocated the humane treatment of slaves, he saw nothing wrong in owning some on his plantation in **South Carolina**.

George Whitefield

Whitefield was a man of extraordinary energy whose preaching engaged people from all walks of life. He died in Newburyport, Massachusetts, near the end of one of his frequent tours of the colonies.

John Winthrop

One of the most important scientists of his age, **John Winthrop** was born in Boston, into a family where relatives were already pursuing scientific careers. Winthrop graduated from **Harvard College** in 1735, and three years later he became a professor of mathematics and natural science at the school, a post he held to the end of his life. During the next 41 years Winthrop not only taught, but he gave many public lectures and demonstrations. In effect, he laid the basis for serious scientific thought and investigations in America.

Winthrop's major work involved astronomy. He was the first person in the colonies to make observations of sunspots. He made valu-able contributions to the questions raised by the *transits* (movements) of Mercury and Venus across the sun, and in 1761 he was responsible for sending an expedition to Newfoundland to observe the transit of Venus. He was one of the first to predict the return of **Halley's Comet**. In addition, he made numerous valuable observations of eclipses and other astronomical phenomena.

Winthrop took as active interest in, and made various contributions to, other areas of science. He was one of the first to support Benjamin Franklin's theories about electricity when many people remained skeptical. Winthrop also carried on observations of magnetism, and made meteorological observations, keeping a detailed record of the weather in **Cambridge** from 1742 to his final days. In 1746 he established the first laboratory of experimental physics in the colonies, and over the years conducted demonstrations of the laws of mechanics, light, and heat.

As a scientific thinker, Winthrop was a progressive in religion and politics. He attacked the traditional notions of the relation of God to creation, and maintained that physical phenomena were the result of natural causes.

Winthrop and his work did not go unrecognized in his day. He published in the most important scientific journals, and was elected to the most prestigious scientific society of the age, **London's Royal Society**. Despite his strong ties to England, Winthrop was a strong supporter of American independence, and even served in some administrative capacities during the early years of the **Revolutionary War**. In every way, John Winthrop was one of the bright lights of the colonies and a beacon of inspiration to America's scientific and intellectual community.

Americans tend to think that Daniel Boone was the first person to explore Kentucky and "open up the west," but **Thomas Walker**—explorer, physician, and Revolutionary patriot—actually got there first. Born in King and Queen County Virginia, Walker studied medicine with his sister's husband; later he moved first to Williamsburg and then to **Fredericksburg**, where he became noted for his skill as a surgeon.

In addition to his medical practice, Walker ran a general store, and began to become interested in trade. His marriage to Mildred Thornton, a wealthy widow, brought him the 11,000-acre Castle Hill estate in Albemarle County.

In 1749, the Loyal Land Company was organized in England. Like the Ohio Company, the Loyal Land Company was designed to open the way through the **Appalachian Mountains** so settlers could move away from the coastal and Piedmont areas in the South. Walker was appointed chief agent for the company, and he was authorized to explore the Appalachian Mountains.

Accompanied by five other men, Walker went into the mountains in the spring of 1750. They discovered a natural opening in the mountains which they named for the British Duke of Cumberland who had won the Battle of Culloden in Scotland four years earlier. To this day **Cumberland Gap** remains an important icon in the opening of the trans-Appalachian west.

Walker and his companions journeyed on. They named the Cumberland River and two of the men built the first log cabin raised by whites between the Cumberland and Ohio Rivers. After surviving numerous escapades—such as bear bites, rattlesnakes, and a charging buffalo—Walker and his companions returned to Virginia. There they found that the Loyal Land Company had been dissolved, and that all their work had been for nothing.

Walker went on to serve in the Virginia **House of Burgesses** in 1752, and then again from 1756 until 1761. He built a proud homestead at Castle Hill, where he was a neighbor of Peter Jefferson, father of the future president. Walker served briefly as a guardian for the young Thomas.

Walker served as an interpreter at several important treaties made with Native American tribes. He represented Virginia at the important **Treaty of Fort Stanwix** in 1768.

When the American Revolution began, Walker showed himself to be an ardent patriot. He served on the Virginia Committee of Safety in 1776 and was a member of the Virginia executive council between 1776 and 1781.

The Cumberland Gap

Jeffrey Amherst was born in the county of Kent in southern England, the son of a well-to-do attorney. At age 14, Jeffrey enlisted in the army, and during the next 25 years, he saw action with the British forces fighting on the Continent—serving in both the War of the Austrian Succession and later the **Seven Years' War**. By 1756, he had attained the rank of colonel and had a reputation as a very capable leader.

The Seven Years' War was also fought in North America, where it was known as the French and Indian War. In 1758, Amherst was promoted to major-general and given command of a major British expedition sent to America and assigned to capture the French fortress of Louisbourg on **Cape Breton Island**, Nova Scotia. He arrived off Louisbourg in May 1758, and by July had forced the French to surrender. As a result, Amherst became an instant hero throughout the British colonies, his name given to towns and counties from New Hampshire to Virginia.

In 1759, Amherst led a large force north from Albany, New York and captured the French forts at **Ticonderoga** and Crown Point. However, he was criticized for not pushing further north that year; as a result most of the laurels for the capture of French Canada went to General **James Wolfe**. In 1760, Amherst masterminded the complicated three-pronged assault that culminated in the surrender of Montreal. The following year Amherst was made a Knight of the Bath, one of England's highest honors.

After the fall of Montreal, Amherst was appointed governor-general of British North America. In 1763, he took command of Pontiac's War, an uprising led by the Indian chief **Pontiac** to resist the British takeover of the forts and territories across the northeast that had formerly been under French control.

Amherst initially underestimated the Indian threat; however, eventually he sent reinforcements to relieve two strategically important forts, and the rebellion collapsed soon after.

Amherst returned to England in 1764, having become disenchanted with life in the colonies. For the next several years, he served in various top government and military posts, including chief military advisor to King **George III**. In 1775, he refused an offer from the king to take command of British troops in America to fight in the Revolutionary War, but he was a strong supporter of fighting the war against the colonists. As late as 1793—at 76 years old—Amherst was still serving the Crown as a military leader, as commander-in-chief of all British forces in England.

Jeffrey Amherst

91. Pontiac
(c. 1720–1769)

The early life of **Pontiac** remains a mystery. It is believed that he was born near the Maumee River in Ohio. What is known is that he became a sachem (chief) of the **Ottawa** tribe around 1755, and made his first appearance in written history as the "Sachem of the Outawawas" reported by Major **Robert Rogers** in 1760. At this time Pontiac was an ally of the French in their war against the British.

As part of the terms of the treaty ending the French and Indian War, the British were to take possession of the French forts, trading posts, and settlements across Ohio, Illinois, and Indiana. The Native Americans of this region had become accustomed to the French, and they did not like the more restrictive demands made on them by the British. Sometime around 1762 or 1763, a Delaware Indian holy man named **Neolin the Prophet**, began to stir up the Indians against all white settlers. Pontiac adopted this message and he convinced many Native Americans that the British alone, and not the French, were the enemy.

Pontiac appeared at the British-held **Fort Detroit** with several hundred warriors in May, 1763. At first, he planned to lead a surprise attack on the fort, but canceled it at the last moment when it was clear that the British knew of the plan. Instead, Pontiac and his men then surrounded the fort and held it under siege for five months, until the end of October.

Pontiac then left, but other Native Americans continued the siege until August 1764.

During the intervening months, native warriors attacked and captured a number of British forts from Detroit, along the Great Lakes, down to modern-day Pittsburgh. Altogether these attacks cost the British forces and colonists several hundred lives.

When he abandoned the siege of Fort Detroit, Pontiac apparently tried to organize other Native Americans in the Mississippi Valley to attack the British. In any case, the war ground to a halt after both Fort Detroit and **Fort Pitt**, at modern-day Pittsburgh, were relieved and resupplied by British forces. In August 1765, Pontiac reappeared at Fort Detroit and smoked a peace pipe with George Croghan, the Indian agent. In July 1766, Pontiac met Sir **William Johnson** at Fort Ontario in Oswego, New York, and signed a treaty formally ending hostilities.

Pontiac lived quietly and peacefully for the next three years. Then in 1769, during a visit to Cahokia, Illinois, he was attacked and killed by a Peoria Indian. The reason for the attack is unknown.

Chief Pontiac united tribes

The Native American warrior and frontier diplomat **Cornstalk** was a member of the Maquachake division of the **Shawnee** tribe. He was born in western Pennsylvania around 1720. We know almost nothing about his early life, but he most likely moved west with most of the Shawnee tribe to modern-day Ohio.

Cornstalk fought on the side of the French against the colonists during the French and Indian War. He led a raid against English settlers in Rockbridge County, Virginia in 1759. Then, during **Pontiac's War**, he led raids in the Greenbriar area of Virginia.

After Pontiac's warriors were defeated in 1763, British Colonel **Henry Bouquet** took a number of Native Americans—including Cornstalk—as hostages to Fort Pitt, at modern-day Pittsburgh. It is uncertain whether Cornstalk escaped from Fort Pitt, or whether he was eventually released. He next appeared in 1774, when clashes between Native Americans and white settlers along the Ohio River frontier threatened to develop into a full-scale war.

Cornstalk wrote to the British governors of Virginia, Pennsylvania, and Maryland, asking for a cessation of hostilities. His answer came in the form of an attack force led by **John Murray**, governor of Virginia.

In the councils that followed, Cornstalk spoke for peace. However, when the Shawnee voted for war, Cornstalk agreed to lead his Maquachake warriors to battle. On October 10, 1774, Cornstalk and his followers fought in the **Battle of Point Pleasant**, in present-day West Virginia. Despite an energetic and imagi-native attack plan, Cornstalk and his men were defeated.

At a meeting with Governor Murray, Cornstalk agreed to accept the Ohio River as the southern boundary of the Shawnee tribe. Cornstalk then went into retirement.

The start of the **American Revolution** brought Cornstalk back to public life. He encouraged his tribesmen to remain neutral, and he made many gestures of good will toward the new United States government. In 1777, he went to American **Fort Randolph**—the site of the Battle of Point Pleasant—to warn the garrison there of potential Indian attacks stirred up by British agents. Cornstalk was held prisoner at the fort, and when an American soldier was shot and killed in an ambush, Cornstalk, his son, and several other Native Americans were brutally murdered by the garrison. Some of the murderers fled; the others were tried and acquitted.

Cornstalk's murder led to nearly 20 years of fighting between the Shawnee and the white Americans. He had worked valiantly over the years in an effort to bring peace between his people and the English settlers—but the hatred and mistrust on both sides was too much to overcome.

Colonists fighting with Indians

The cultivation of indigo

Elizabeth Lucas was born in the Caribbean, on the island of Antigua, in the British West Indies. The daughter of a British official and army officer, Elizabeth was educated in England, before her father moved his family to the **South Carolina** Colony in 1738. They settled on the Wappoo River, near the capital of Charles Town.

Lieutenant Colonel Lucas went to England in 1739, leaving his young daughter in charge of her ailing mother as well as the main plantation at Wappoo and two other family properties. Eliza, as she was usually called, responded swiftly to the new responsibilities; she became known as one of the most efficient and charming plantation mistresses in the colony.

Eliza Lucas began to experiment with indigo seeds in 1741. Up to this time, rice had been the principal crop for the South Carolina Colony. Eliza had only moderate success at first. However, with the assistance of an experienced planter her father sent from the Caribbean, by 1744, Lucas had successfully ripened **indigo** seeds. She sent her first indigo shipment—six pounds—to England in 1747. By 1774, the year prior to the **American Revolution**, the export had risen to an amazing 1,107,660 pounds.

In 1744, Lucas married **Charles Pinckney**, a widower who was twice her age. He built the Belmont plantation on **Charles Town Neck** and the couple lived in prosperity and social distinction.

Pinckeny was appointed the colonial agent for South Carolina in 1753 and the family moved to England. Charles Pinckney died in 1758, and Eliza returned to South Carolina. She left her two sons in England to receive their education, and did not see them again until the start of the American Revolution. Though they were schooled in Britain, the sons sided with the **Patriot** cause, served with distinction during the war, and then went on to fill important positions during the early Federal period.

Eliza's later years were spent with her family. She lived at the family property at Belmont until 1783, when she went to live with her widowed daughter and her grandchildren at the plantation on the Santee River. During these years, Eliza also became a good friend of **George Washington**; when she died in Philadelphia at the age of 71, at his own request, President Washington served as one of the pallbearers at her funeral.

94. Samuel Adams
(1722-1803)

Today we think of him as the firebrand and agitator of pre-Revolutionary Boston. However, **Samuel Adams** thought of himself as a "patriot" in the old-fashioned meaning of the word; he wanted to defend the ancient rights and privileges of British subjects. How he evolved into a new American "Patriot" is the story of his life and career.

Adams was born in Boston in 1722. He entered Harvard College at age 14, and graduated when he was only 18. He stayed at Harvard to write a master's thesis inspired by John Locke's theories of the compact that exists between the rulers and those who are governed.

Although his family thought he should become a minister, Adams drifted slowly but surely into politics. He was elected to the Massachusetts legislature in 1765 and served until 1774. During this time he helped organize the **Sons of Liberty**, the secret organization of colonists that sprang up in protest of Parliament's passage of the **Stamp Act** of 1765. Adams became one of the men who organized boycotts and demonstrations against what they considered to be the tyranny of "taxation without representation." These men saw King **George III** and his ministers as the problem, and looked to Parliament for redress of their grievances. When that did not come, Adams began to turn to thoughts of freedom and independence.

In 1773, Adams organized the most famous act of defiance in pre-Revolutionary Massachusetts—the **Boston Tea Party**—to protest the Tea Act. When British soldiers and American militiamen fired upon one another at Lexington and Concord on April 19, 1775, Adams—along with **Patrick Henry** and John Hancock—became one of the most visible leaders of the movement for independence.

Adams was a member of both the First and Second Continental Congresses (1774-1781), and signed the Declaration of Independence; however, he spent much of the Revolutionary years in the background. His cousin, **John Adams**, took the lead of the Massachusetts delegation to the Second Continental Congress, and Samuel returned to Boston in 1781.

Adams played an important role in shaping the Massachusetts state constitution, which was approved in 1780. Although he had grown up in colonial Massachusetts, shaped by merchants and ministers, he encouraged the drafters of the document to provide for social equality and religious freedom. Adams later served as governor of Massachusetts between 1794 and 1797.

When he died in 1803, Massachusetts mourned the loss of her native son who had fought for the traditional liberties of an Englishman, but who had played a great role in forming a new nation—one without a king, an aristocracy, or one established church.

Samuel Adams

95. Crispus Attucks
(c. 1723–1770)

The Boston Massacre

Very little is known about the life of **Crispus Attucks** until the time just prior to his death in the **Boston Massacre** of March 5, 1770. Evidence suggests that he was regarded as a black man; however, whether he was entirely of African descent, of mixed white-African heritage, or mixed African-American Indian descent is uncertain. Attucks is believed to have been a runaway slave who apparently managed to live the life of a free man by working on the Boston waterfront or possibly sailing on ships.

By the year 1770, there was increasing friction between the people of Boston and the British soldiers quartered among them to maintain order. On the night of March 5, a crowd of Bostonians began to throw snowballs at the small British guard unit at the **Custom House** across from the State House. As the crowd became more threatening, the British called for more troops. At the same time, church bells began to ring announcing that there was some sort of emergency.

Attucks was eating his supper with other sailors and harbor workers at a tavern when the sound of the bells reached them. Rumors had also quickly spread that the British troops were planning some hostile action. Attucks left the tavern, somewhere picked up a large wooden club, and along with some 20 to 30 other men made his way to the Custom House square.

By the time Attucks arrived, British Captain **Thomas Preston** was also there with a small relief force of British troops. The crowd had grown and was now even more unruly. Some Bostonians were trying to calm things down, but there was simply too much confusion. Some in the crowd were daring the British to fire on them. Preston was doing his best to keep his men from firing, but there were now open scuffles involving his men and the colonists. Whether someone in the crowd shouted "Fire!" or the soldiers simply lost control under fear, shots were fired.

Among those hit was Attucks; he took two bullets in his chest, fell to the ground and died. In less than two minutes, five colonists were either dead or mortally wounded.

In the trial of the British troops, Attucks was often singled out by the prosecution as an innocent martyr and by the defense as a prime agitator. Most likely he was neither. However, by choosing to pick up a club and put himself in the front line, he must have been motivated by some hatred of the British. To that extent, Crispus Attucks was one of the first patriots who died in the battle for American independence.

96. Gaspar de Portola
(c. 1723–1784)

Gaspar de Portola was born into a noble family in Catalonia, Spain. The first historical record of his life is his enlistment in the Spanish army in the 1730s. He served Spain for the next 30 years, rising to the rank of captain while fighting in Italy and Portugal. In 1767 he was sent to serve as governor of the province of **California**.

Portola's most important assignment was to establish a Spanish presence in upper California, preferably at a site reported by the Spanish explorer **Sebastian Vizcaino** in 1603. The Spanish were becoming concerned that the English and the Russians would come down from the north and seize parts of California.

Portola arrived in Mexico and set about organizing an expedition. It was to have four units; two detachments would go by sea and two others would proceed over land. Two ships left **Lower California** (modern-day Baja California) early in 1769. The first land party left Velicanta in Lower California in March. Portola set out with the second detachment in May.

Traveling with Portola was **Junipero Serra**, a Franciscan priest (see no. 85). By the end of June, Portola had reached the point near what would one day become **San Diego**; the other three detachments soon joined his party. Portola established the first of many presidios—military forts—in California, and Father Serra founded the first of many **Franciscan** missions, San Diego de Alcala, on July 16, 1769.

Portola then proceeded northward overland with 40 men. In August they camped near a river they named *Porciuncula*, in honor of Spain's Our Lady the Queen of the Angels of Porciuncula. The area where Portola's camp was established would become the city of **Los Angeles**.

By October, Portola reached the Bay of Monterey; although this was the place reported by Vizcaino, Portola and his party did not realize it. Instead, they continued farther north to **San Francisco**, where his party explored the region; in fact, they were the first white men known to have looked down on San Francisco Bay.

The party turned back, and after a difficult journey arrived in San Diego at the end of January, 1770. By now Portola was convinced that he had found the site reported by Vizcaino, and he made a voyage by ship back to Monterey Bay that May. At nearby **Carmel**, Portola established the presidio on June 3, 1770, and Father Serra founded the mission of San Carlos Borromeo. Six days later Portola sailed back to Mexico. In 1776, he was made governor of the city of **Puebla**, east of Mexico City. Eight years later he died, either in Mexico or in Spain.

Portola discovering the Golden Gate

97. James Wolfe
(1727–1759)

British military hero **James Wolfe** was born in the county of Kent, in southern England and educated at the military school at Greenwich. At age 14, he was commissioned a second lieutenant in his father's regiment of marines. Over the years, as Wolfe rose in rank, and he gained a reputation as a highly competent officer. He stood out as a leader who was willing to take aggressive action, and wasn't afraid to criticize the failings of his fellow officers.

It was the former quality that brought him to the attention of Britain's prime minister, **William Pitt**. In 1758, Pitt named Wolfe to command a brigade in the planned assault on the French fort of Louisbourg, **Cape Breton**, Nova Scotia. This was the major expedition led by **Jeffrey Amherst**. Wolfe played an important role in the successful landing and then siege of Louisbourg that ended in the surrender of the French fortress in July, 1758.

Wolfe was promoted to major general, and assigned to command the British forces that were to sail up the **St. Lawrence River** and capture the city of Quebec. This was part of a three-pronged attack in which Amherst was to march overland from upstate New York, and another British force was to sail down the St. Lawrence. Neither of these forces ever made it to **Quebec**.

By June, 1759, Wolfe had brought some 9,000 men to the Isle of Orleans, four miles below Quebec. In the weeks that followed, his forces made several attempts to approach the well defended city. Finally during the night of September 12-13, Wolfe launched his most audacious attack. Although he was weak from illness, he personally led 4,500 of his men to climb the steep cliffs that brought them to the heights above Quebec City. From there he advanced onto the **Plains of Abraham**, a flat area only about a mile away.

The next morning, the French, led by General **Louis-Joseph Montcalm**, were stunned to see the British drawn up and ready for battle. Montcalm attacked with around 4,500 men. The British fought aggressively, and in the battle Wolfe was severely wounded. He was taken to the rear by his troops, where he continued to give orders to pursue the French. Near the end, it was said that he asked, "Who runs?" When his men assured him that it was the French, Wolfe is said to have replied, "Now God be praised, since I have conquered, I will die in peace."

Wolfe was given the honor that Britain grants her greatest heroes— a monument in **Westminster Abbey**. His death on the field of battle was depicted by several famous painters, including the American artist Benjamin West.

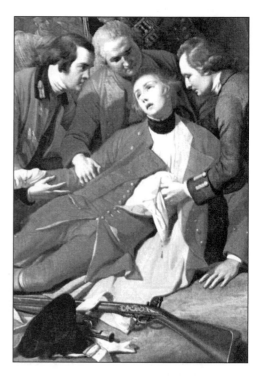

The death of James Wolfe

98. Robert Rogers
(1731–1795)

A true soldier of fortune, **Robert Rogers** was born in Methuen, Massachusetts, and grew up on the New Hampshire frontier. Six feet tall and gifted with great physical endurance, he became known for his skill in the woods.

When the French and Indian War began in 1754, Rogers worked as a recruiting officer. In 1756, he became captain of an independent company of rangers. "**Rogers's Rangers**" soon became famous for their exploits against the **Abenaki Indians**, who were allied with the French. In October 1759, Rogers led his men on their most daring mission. They crossed the border into French Canada and nearly destroyed the Abenaki settlement of St. Francis on the south side of the **St. Lawrence River**. At the age of 29, Rogers had become the most celebrated fighter in the American colonies.

In 1761, Rogers married Elizabeth Browne of Portsmouth, New Hampshire. For the next four years, Rogers continued to battle Indians on the frontier. In 1765, he resigned his commission and went to England. There, he published his memoirs and produced a play about his adventures in the colonies. His writings show that he was a sharp and sympathetic observer of the American Indians.

Rogers returned to America and served as commandant of **Fort Michilimackinac,** between Lakes Michigan and Huron from 1766 to 1768. However, he was dismissed from that post after being accused of treason for dealing with the French. He was tried and acquitted; he then returned to London, seeking to revive his fortunes.

Things went from bad to worse. Plagued by financial problems throughout his life, Rogers was soon thrown into London's debtors' prison. He remained there for 22 months, and emerged from jail a man broken both in health and spirit.

Robert Rogers

Rogers returned to North America in 1775, just at the start of the **American Revolution**. After a brief reunion in Portsmouth, his wife sent him away and began divorce proceedings. He never saw her or their son again.

General George Washington distrusted Rogers and had him briefly imprisoned as a spy for the British. This turned Rogers into a true **Loyalist**. He joined the British side and became commander of the **Queen's American Rangers**, a regiment of Tories. He was defeated at White Plains, New York in 1776 and was removed from command in 1777.

Rogers fled to England in 1780. He spent more time in debtors' prisons and died alone in a lodging house in London. It was a tragic end for a brave, military hero and frontier adventurer.

Paul Revere
(1735–1818)

Paul Revere

America's most famous messenger was born in Boston, Massachusetts to Appollos Revoire (a Huguenot who had escaped persecution in France) and Deborah Hitchbourne. **Paul Revere** (the name was changed to accommodate English-American culture) received a basic education in Boston schools and then worked in his father's silversmith trade. He saw his first military service in 1756, when he joined an expedition against Fort Crown Point in New York during the French and Indian War.

He set up his silversmith shop, became a Freemason, and came to associate with prominent Bostonians such as **John Adams,**

Samuel Adams (see no. 94), and **Joseph Warren**. It is not certain when he became a confirmed patriot. However, in 1770, he did an engraving of the **Boston Massacre**, a picture that clearly showed his sympathies toward the growing cause of freedom for the colonies. After becoming a leader of the Boston **Sons of Liberty**, he participated in the **Boston Tea Party** and became a dispatch rider for the Boston Committee of Safety.

During 1774, Revere rode to Philadelphia, Pennsylvania and Portsmouth, New Hampshire on a number of important missions for the Committee of Safety. His most famous service, however, took place during the night hours of April 18-19, 1775. Having learned that British General **Thomas Gage** was sending troops out of Boston to arrest Samuel Adams and **John Hancock**, as well as to confiscate the patriot stores of ammunition at Concord, revere was sent by the Committee to warn of the British plan. After being rowed across the Charles River to Charlestown, he rode to Concord, possibly crying out, "The British are coming!" to homes along his route. Revere never made it to concord. He was detained by British patrols after he left Lexington. **Dr. Samuel Prescott** was the dispatch rider who reached and alerted the town of Concord. Nevertheless, Revere's ride was commemorated in **Henry Wadsworth Longfellow's** poem in 1863, and became an important part of the mystique of the American Revolution.

Revere went back to silversmithing, designed the Massachusetts state seal, and molded much of the hardware for the frigate USS Constitution. A Federalist in his politics, he wore the clothing typical of the Revolutionary era until his death; it had gone out of style 20 years earlier. He was buried in the Granary Burial Ground in Boston.

Remembered today in New Orleans and along the Gulf of Mexico, **Bernardo de Gálvez** was the most energetic and successful of the governors of Spanish Louisiana. He helped the American patriots during the **Revolutionary War**, and he restored a measure of glory to the Spanish Empire in North America.

Gálvez was born in Malaga, Spain in 1746. His father and his uncle were both prominent court officials. Galvez entered the Spanish army as a lieutenant and was promoted to captain in 1762. Three years later, he went to Mexico with his uncle, **Jose de Gálvez**, who had been appointed minister-general of the province of **New Spain** (Mexico.)

Gálvez fought in a campaign against the **Apache Indians** along the Rio Grande in 1770. He returned to Spain in 1775, and was promoted to lieutenant colonel after he was wounded in a Spanish campaign in Africa. Gálvez was sent to **Spanish Louisiana** in 1776, and was named acting governor in January, 1777.

In November, 1777 Gálvez married Felicite Destrehan, a widowed daughter of a prominent French Creole family. The marriage quickly gained him the affection and loyalty of the native Creole population of **New Orleans**.

Gálvez favored the American colonies in their struggle for independence. He channeled

Bernardo de Gálvez

funds to American frontier forces fighting in the Illinois country. When Spain declared war on Great Britain in May, 1779, Gálvez mobilized forces to eject the British from their forts on the **Mississippi River** and the Gulf of Mexico.

Two hurricanes—one in August, 1779 and the other in October, 1780—scattered Gálvez's fleets; however, he remained undaunted. His forces occupied the British fort at Mobile in 1780, and captured the well-defended fort at **Pensacola**, Florida after a four-month siege in 1781. By the time the war ended, Gálvez had captured the entire British province of West Florida. King **Charles III** of Spain awarded him a royal title with the motto, A Yo Solo (I Alone) on his coat of arms.

As a reward for his military exploits, Gálvez was made Viceroy of New Spain in 1785; he arrived with his wife and three children in early 1786. Gálvez began a new policy toward the Indians, doing away with the old solutions of building presidios and missions, and replacing them with the idea of tying the Indians to the Spanish through economic and technological dependence. However, he became seriously ill with fever in 1786, and died before he could see his new ideas carried out. Galveston Bay and **Galveston**, Texas are named in Gálvez's honor, and he is commemorated in New Orleans with a statue.

TRIVIA QUIZ & PROJECTS

Test your knowledge and challenge your friends with the following questions. The answers are on the biographies noted.

1. Who searched for a magical spring with waters that supposedly restored one's youth and wound up discovering Florida? (see no. 2)

2. Which Indian warrior replaced his half brother as tribal chief and led a series of organized attacks that killed almost one-third of the Virginia colony? (see no. 12)

3. Who became the chief intermediary and interpreter between the Wampanoag Indians and the first Pilgrims to settle in Plymouth in 1621? (see no. 17)

4. Which Indian princess supposedly saved a colonist's life, converted to Christianity, and married an English adventurer? (see no. 30)

5. Why did a religious leader banished from the Massachusetts Bay colony in 1635 establish a new colony? (see no. 35)

6. Which energetic and able governor of the New Netherland colony was nicknamed "Old Silver-Leg?" (see no. 42)

7. What river did two famous French explorers reach in June, 1673? (see no. 48)

8. Who was responsible for the greatest moment of French explorations in North America? (see no. 53)

9. How did a famous colonial woman escape from her Indian captors after she had been taken prisoner? (see no. 62)

10. Which famous colonial doctor was credited with saving many lives during a smallpox epidemic? (see. no. 70)

11. Which member of the English Parliament founded the colony of Georgia? (see no. 75)

12. Who was the German immigrant who became a pioneer for freedom of the press in the colonies? (see no. 78)

13. How did the Spanish establish several missions in California during the 18th century? (see no. 85)

14. Which colonial woman first developed indigo as a major crop in South Carolina? (see no. 93)

15. Why did a famous American-born soldier-of-fortune remain a Loyalist and fight on the British side during the Revolutionary War? (see no. 98)

Suggested Projects

1. Choose one of the leaders from this book—either a colonist, explorer, or Native American—and write a diary entry for that person that describes in detail one of the most significant days or incidents in that person's life.

2. By 1763, the British had driven both the French and the Spanish out of all of North America. Twelve years later, the American colonists went to war and declared their independence from Great Britain. However, suppose the French and their Indian allies had fought the British to a stalemate in the French and Indian War. Suppose the French could have maintained a presence in Canada, and continued to explore the continent west of the Appalachian Mountains. What do you think would have happened to the colonies? Would they have still broken away from Great Britain? Would the French have founded other colonies to the west and south of the existing ones? How might that have affected life in places such as Virginia, Massachusetts, and New York? Write a brief essay describing how things might have been different if the British and the colonists had not won the French and Indian War.

Index

Index

Index

Index